Alvin Mitchell
July 6, 1959
Wooster, Ohio

Resources for Sermon Preparation

Books by David A. MacLennan
Published by The Westminster Press

RESOURCES FOR SERMON PREPARATION
ENTRUSTED WITH THE GOSPEL
PASTORAL PREACHING

Resources for Sermon Preparation

by

DAVID A. MacLENNAN

Philadelphia
THE WESTMINSTER PRESS

Scripture quotations used by permission are from: *The Revised Standard Version of the Bible,* copyright, 1946 and 1952, by the Division of Christian Education of the National Council of Churches; *The Bible: A New Translation,* by James Moffatt, copyright, 1922, 1935, and 1950, by Harper & Brothers; *Letters to Young Churches,* by J. B. Phillips, copyright by The Macmillan Company, 1947, and *The Gospels,* by J. B. Phillips, copyright by The Macmillan Company, 1952. The quotations from G. K. Chesterton, Ogden Nash, Robert Freeman, John Masefield, and G. A. Studdert-Kennedy are used by permission.

LIBRARY OF CONGRESS CATALOG CARD NO.: 57–9604

PRINTED IN THE UNITED STATES OF AMERICA

CONTENTS

PREFACE

At the Study Door

David Lloyd George, sometime prime minister of Great Britain, once spoke to the late Dr. James Black, the eminent Edinburgh preacher, concerning preaching. As an eloquent political speaker, the gifted Welshman contrasted his task with that of the parish minister. "I don't know how you ministers do it. . . . I don't need to create my own atmosphere: it is there before me, electric and buoyant; my audience cheers the tritest remark or the most inane joke. But you are in the same place, speaking to the same people, twice a Sunday. The people don't come expecting fireworks or to be amused. And you have to speak, by and large, always on the same subject, and you have to stir or create your own atmosphere. I think that to be a minister in a settled church is one of the hardest arts of speaking known to me."

To preach even once a week on the same glorious subject to the same people is one of the most exacting arts, as it is one of the highest of all vocations. Every Christian preacher has inexhaustible resources. Despite his inadequacy, to him is entrusted the enduring gospel. To Christ's herald is given the inspiration and illumination of the Holy Spirit, without whom we are "noisy gongs" and "clanging cymbals," full of sound and signifying nothing. Nevertheless there comes to the most faithful transmitter of the Word arid stretches on his homiletical pilgrimage. As we say in our professional idiom, "the well is dry," or "the pump needs priming." To help to provide "priming" I have contributed a monthly article to the magazine *Church Management.* This book is based on the material used in my columns.

Every preacher of the good news of Christ rightly rejects packaged homilies. To thaw out and warm up frozen food for men's minds and souls exactly as prepared by another is distasteful to dispenser and recipient alike. In addition, the sheep that look up may not be fed a sufficiently fresh diet. Therefore the following pages provide recipes, and, it is to be hoped, insights and ideas whereby the Bread of Life may be given to our people. These resources for sermon preparation are not apt to prove useful without the effort of the good " workman who has no need to be ashamed, rightly handling the word of truth " (II Tim. 2:15). But these suggestions are offered to my conscientious and busy brothers in Christ's service in the hope that they may be stimulated to produce what our Lord called " the food which endures to eternal life " (John 6:27).

To Dr. William H. Leach, editor in chief, and to Mr. Edwin A. Lane, managing editor of *Church Management,* I give my appreciation for their encouragement to me since I joined their friendly and competent team. By their permission I use material that originally appeared in their publication. To Charles L. Wallis, of Keuka College, Keuka Park, New York, I am indebted for editorial suggestions. I wish also to thank Miss Barbara Chatfield, of Yale University, and Mrs. Alexander D. Dunbar, my secretary, for their helpfulness in the preparation of the manuscript. Many others should receive bouquets of gratitude, including the staff of The Westminster Press. To my wife, as always, I owe an unpayable debt for her gentle and persistent urging to commit the " priming " to print.

David A. MacLennan

Brick Presbyterian Church
Rochester, New York

I

ADVENT

Season of Expectancy

ADVENT

How the Word Gets Through

" You are as young as your words! " I quote a competent psychologist and esteemed writer, Mrs. Bonaro W. Overstreet, from her book *How to Stay Alive as Long as You Live.* Chapter III is devoted to the proposition that the words we use in daily conversation tell our psychological age. " If we are mental and emotional infants, our own words give us away. If our spirits are already doddering while our bodies are yet vigorous, our words declare that fact."

When are words lively and " eternally young "? Mrs. Overstreet's answer is persuasive: " Words have life in them and are eternally young when they tell us unmistakably that back of them lies a vivid encounter with life. Words are old and dull and tired when all they have to report is timeworn, secondhand experience."

Inevitably a discussion of words brings to the Christian mind the thought of the Word, the divine word made flesh in our Lord Jesus Christ. Advent is the season of expectation and preparation for Him who is both ancient of days and eternally the " young prince of glory."

In his serious and needed study of the church, *The Strangeness of the Church,* Daniel Jenkins has reminded us that " the fundamental meaning [of the Word] is God's speech to man, what God says when he addresses man. This is ' the word of the Lord ' which came to the prophet. It is summed up in Jesus Christ, God's decisive Word." He discusses how the word of God comes to us through our Scriptures, and then says that because God's word is living, " it does not remain incarcerated within the pages of Scripture or in the past history of the church. Jesus Christ in the Spirit speaks to his people now." When we wait with others upon the living Lord in the mysterious activity we call worship, then as a church we hear the word of God by which the church lives.

During Advent you might preach a series on " How the Word Gets Through ": (1) in the prophets, (2) in the sacraments, (3) in the Bible, (4) in our Lord Jesus, " who came as at this time." We might find ourselves toiling more strenuously as we try to communicate understandably and vividly the Christian belief concerning God's revelation and supreme incarnation. But no one, least of all our Lord, ever promised that his service would be easy. And our people might find Christmas to be much more than our superficial celebrations indicate.

Self-expression — God's Problem Too

At the beginning God expressed Himself. That Personal Expression was with God and was God, and He existed with God from the beginning. . . . So the Expression of God became a human being and lived among us. We saw His splendour.

JOHN 1: 1-2, 14 (PHILLIPS).

Human beings often find significant self-expression to be a baffling problem. Sometimes, even yet, so-called progressive parents excuse tantrums on the part of Junior by saying, " He's just expressing himself." Until a personality achieves a measure of satisfying expression, self-realization and its accompanying joy are denied.

Is it fantastic or presumptuous to imagine that the infinite personality — God himself — sought and seeks self-expression for our sakes more than his own? Christmas celebrates God's most perfect self-expression, his incarnation in a human personality " born of woman, born under the law," Jesus Christ. What the

Greeks termed the *logos,* or the divine word, sought and found expression in the Man Christ Jesus. Rightly, therefore, has the modern translator J. B. Phillips used the phrase that is more meaningful to twentieth-century folk than *logos,* or " word ": " Personal Expression."

Jesus, the Lord of Christians, is God's self-expression, not one man's achievement. In *Christian Faith To-Day,* Bishop Stephen Neill says:

" Over and over again the New Testament makes it clear that Jesus of Nazareth is to be regarded, not as a product of natural development from within humanity, but as a new power from God, through which a wholly new beginning was made in the history of the world. 'Ye know the grace of our Lord Jesus Christ, that, though he was rich, yet for your sakes he became poor, that ye through his poverty might be rich' (II Cor. 8: 9). These words of Saint Paul are unintelligible, if Jesus is regarded as no more than the highest stage yet reached in the upward progress of man toward God."

Christian thinkers tried one term after another to express their understanding of what Jesus had done for men — Prophet, Messiah, Servant of the Lord, Captain of Salvation, Son of God — and then adopted the Greek word *logos,* " the word," to set forth their deepest understanding of the truth. Reaching back to the Old Testament to that word by which creation began, and reaching back into Greek philosophy, where the word meant reason in the universe and in man, the best modern English equivalent may be " self-expression " or " revelation." God in his being remains an unfathomable mystery, but it is his nature to be self-revealing. So the Scripture verses that follow — and are used in this way by Bishop Neill — set forth four ways or modes in which the infinite God expressed himself, made himself known so that our little minds could grasp something of the divine meaning, and our little hearts draw near and adore him.

I. *The Word was power.* " All things were made through him " (John 1:3). Also see Rom. 1:20.

II. *The Word was light.* " In him was life, and the life was the light of men " (John 1:4): light upon the nature of being; light upon questions of right and wrong; light upon life and death, the ultimate questions.

III. *The Word was speech.* " There was a man sent from God, whose name was John " (John 1:6). John stood in the line of the prophets, those God-intoxicated souls who were convinced that the word of God dwelt in them and that they must speak it. Therefore, it was to them neither untrue nor presumptuous to say, " Thus saith the Lord." Men's consciences confirmed that what the prophets said as God's message was indeed God's truth.

IV. *The Word was man.* " The Word became flesh and dwelt among us," or using Phillips' translation, " So the Expression of God became a human being and lived among us. We saw His splendour (the splendour, as of the Father's only Son), full of grace and truth " (John 1:14).

The word " flesh " means human nature, in all its limitations and possibilities. Bishop Neill writes:

" This is the final state of the self-revelation of God; the everlasting *Logos* makes himself perfectly one with the human race under the conditions of human life as it is lived by men. Beyond that perfect self-identification no further step in self-identification can ever be imagined, and this is therefore the term and crown of the self-disclosure of God to men."

God's Dream

You and I may not read the Apocrypha, but the " testament between the Testaments " repays reading. Preaching as well as historical and devotional values are to be found in many of its passages. When the RSV committee publishes its new English version, wise preachers will explore the now relatively unknown Scriptures considered by most Protestant scholars to be below the level of the books in our Old and New Testaments. One unforgettable passage leaps out of the Second Book of the Maccabees.

It has preaching possibilities for Advent and Christmas. Judas Maccabaeus, the fiery Robert Bruce of the Jews, is the hero. He is leading the loyalists against the hated occupying army. His troops have little armament and too few "effectives." But the intrepid leader relies on something more powerful. Here is the description of how he equipped them to fight gloriously for their cause:

"And arming each one of them, not so much with the sure defence of shields and spears as with the encouragement that lieth in good words, and moreover relating to them a dream worthy to be believed, he made them all exceeding glad."

Let that phrase sing its way into your imagination: "arming . . . them . . . with . . . a dream worthy to be believed"!

Realists discount dreams. Idealists have repeatedly bungled. But what if the dream is God's dream? Is not this what God did in sending Jesus Christ? The divine dream, the divine thought, expressed itself in a human person who lived on our earth, and "we saw His splendour (the splendour, as of the Father's only Son), full of grace and truth."

What was the nature and intention of this "dream," this hope, this design? First, that you and I and every child of God could be redeemed. Secondly, that human society — this sorry scheme of things — could be redeemed through God's dream-made-real in the life and death and resurrection of Christ. We have God's word for it. Here is the basis of the Christian hope.

As at Evanston in August, 1954, so always, Christian thinkers will argue, speculate, differ, as to the interpretation of Christ the Hope of the World. But all Christians unite in affirming the truth. "We affirm our faith in Jesus Christ as the hope of the world, and desire to share that faith with all men," begins the Message from the World Council of Churches. And the triumphant conclusion reads: "We do not know what is coming to us. But we know who is coming. It is he who meets us every day and who will meet us at the end — Jesus Christ our Lord. Therefore we say to you, Rejoice in hope."

The Divine "Hide-and-Seek"

Verily thou art a God that hidest thyself, O God of Israel, the Saviour.

Isaiah 45: 15.

Have you ever felt that in this universe a cosmic game of "hide-and-seek" is being played? Few need to be persuaded that God exists and that this complex system is not a thing of happenstance. Yet we are unable to see God, to apprehend, to touch him. To many, God is so obscure, vague, and hidden, that for all life-affecting purposes he might as well not exist.

God came out of hiding, so to speak, nineteen centuries ago, and, for the brief lifetime of the Son of his love, unveiled himself. Yet during that self-revelation, Christ said that in a little while he would not be seen. True, the loving and trusting child of God has moments when God seems very near, a presence beside him, a hand near that beckons and upholds. Yet easily the circumstances shift and the vision passes.

> "He hides himself so wondrously
> As if there were no God;
> He is least seen when all the powers
> Of ill are most abroad."
>
> — *F. W. Faber*

This a paradox of the life of the spirit: God hides himself from us even while he discloses himself to us. So says Isa., ch. 45. This is part of the comfort of such an insight. We may have unbreakable confidence and certitude that God is, that he is the creator, sustainer, and redeemer of the universe and of our lives. Yet because we are human, finite creatures, we can never be granted indisputable proof that he is all that Christian experience claims him to be. We are sure, and not sure. "Eye hath not seen, nor ear heard. . . . Now we see through a glass, darkly. . . . Now I know in part. . . . Verily thou art a God that hidest thyself." A. E. Whitham, in *The Pastures of His Presence,* wrote that there is something in this revealed religion of Christ that is "secretive, elusive, hidden; something incalculable, more suggestive than direct, impossible to handle as a snowflake or the perfume of a flower, . . . a thing without edges because without bounds, dark with depth, or blinding with excess of light; simple to know, but mysterious to understand; sure, but not plain."

A preacher who handles this theme may find himself in deep waters, but the venture will be worth-while. God is so much greater than anything we can say about him. Each preacher will develop the sermon in his own way. But two major divisions seem clear:

I. *God is,* and God is the Father of the Lord Jesus Christ. Under this heading we may cite some cogent reasons for this certitude of faith.

II. *God hides himself.* Could he do otherwise and be God? Could he reveal himself clearly to our "naked sight" and not utterly overwhelm us? No man can see God and live. Does he not hide himself for love of us? We must learn to trust where we cannot see. But he has revealed himself sufficiently for us to grasp and rejoice. He hides himself in one sense that he may perfect us, "till we all come in the unity of the faith, and of the knowledge of the Son of God, unto a perfect man, unto the measure of the stature of the fulness of Christ" (Eph. 4:13).

The Christian Hope

You may preach a series of sermons on "The Christian Hope." Advent's four Sundays would be an ideal time to do it. As you know, the season's title was given to the Sundays preceding Christmas to stress the coming of the Lord, both in history and beyond history. An immensely helpful service would be given your people if in such sermons you tried to answer questions many of them ask: How is Christ our Hope? What is meant by saying, "We know who is coming"? Are we to believe that Christ will come "on clouds descending"? Does he come now in judgment and in deliverance? What must we do in the light of this Hope? Christ arms us with "a dream worthy to be believed," which is infinitely more than a dream as we customarily mean it. As Christ's herald, you may help others, now wistful and confused, to find and use his invincible armor.

His Coming

Advent connotes coming. The Sundays before Christmas could be used for a series of sermons on God's advent in history, both B.C. and when in Palestine he intersected time with the birth of his Son Jesus Christ. One sermon could be addressed to the question, "How does God come now?"

Another might bravely face the question to which sincere though misguided people give dogmatic and precise answers which have no warrant in the church's faith: "When will he come again?" A former Presbyterian Moderator was asked by one of his parishioners why he never preached on the Second Coming. He replied, "Because so many people don't seem to have heard of the first coming!" Yet there may be in our community and congregation those who would be helped by an honest, reverent exposition of the church's faith concerning the Second Coming. Such an exposition would have in it both Christian agnosticism concerning the last things and reverent affirmation that "times and seasons" are God's business and knowledge, not ours.

Among the certainties of faith are these: (1) Christ came again in the Holy Spirit (see the Fourth Gospel's statement of Jesus' promises). (2) He comes where "meek souls will receive him." (3) He comes every day in judgment and in mercy. (4) At the end of history he will come as Savior and Judge. Such a sermon will not fail to confront us with the searching query, What must we do in the light of this?

God's Preparation and Ours

Here are four Advent themes celebrating God's preparation and ours: (1) "Hear, O Israel!" (Deut. 6:4). (2) "Rejoice, O Israel! " (Isa., ch. 35). (3) " Turn back, O man! " (Joel 2: 12; Matt. 3: 1-12). (4) " Awake, my soul! " (Rom. 13: 11-14).

The Names of Jesus

Another series of pre-Christmas messages may be based on names or titles of Jesus: (1) Immanuel — " God with Us " (Isa. 7: 14). (2) Wonderful Counselor, Prince of Peace (Isa. 9: 6). (3) Suffering Servant (Isa., chs. 52; 53). (4) Son of David (Matt. 1: 1, 2, 6, 12, 15-17). (5) Son of Mary (Mark 6:3). (6) " Whom say ye that I am? " (Mark 8: 27-30). These were quarried by Joel Miller.

UNIVERSAL BIBLE SUNDAY

Everyman's Book of the Month Club

Does someone sigh, "Not that!" How many book clubs are there? But we need to be active members of the Book of the Ages Club. Some thirty years ago the salvage ship *Artiglio* was working over the sunken ship *Egypt*. Object: gold. As the seekers cleared away debris and mud from the bullion room, a strange object came to light. It looked like part of an old book. Washed and dried topside, a printed page appeared. Those who read English knew that it was a part of the Bible, the story of David and Jonathan. They had sought treasure, and their first discovery was a fragment of the Book of God. Men think the Bible has outlived its usefulness, but, searching for treasure by which to live, they uncover the Bible amid the debris sunk by planetary storms and rediscover its worth. Why a Bible book club? See an apostolic answer in Rom. 15:4, for (1) instruction, (2) steadfastness, (3) encouragement, and (4) hope.

How to Read the Bible

1. Read the Bible regularly. This means daily, even at the sacrifice of a quarter hour of sleep in the morning or one less TV film at night!

2. Read honestly. Try to find out what the passage means, preferably the entire book and then the passage selected from it. What did the writer intend? To whom was he first speaking? What was

the situation or background? What does this message say to me now?

3. Read the Bible in as readable and attractive an edition as you can find.

4. Read imaginatively. " Try," said John Ruskin, " to be present, as if in the body, at each recorded event in the life of the Redeemer." Hear the laughter, or the sobs, echoing through the incident reported and the words spoken.

5. Read with some plan. Follow a scheme or syllabus. Certainly we do well to suggest to new readers that they begin with the earliest Gospel, Mark, for there is no better way to begin Bible study than by " reading Mark straight through without stopping on the route, and by repeating the process until the central figure haunts us like a melody."

6. Read devotionally. Remember that you are moving into a region where One comes to meet you who demands a decision from you, and whose coming brings you all that you could dream of wanting. Reading this book brings travel privileges. You'll find yourself in the Holy Land where Christ is born, and where you will remain with him to the journey's end.

A Sailor's Logbook

My son Mark. 1 PETER 5:13.

Why begin reading the Bible with the Gospels? Because the key to the Bible as the word of God for us is the Word made flesh, who lived among us, Jesus Christ. To gain a strong impression of him during his human life, we need a detailed study of the literature about him.

Why Mark's Gospel first? Because it is earliest, shortest, and most vivid. In it is the good news of God's action in a wholly unique person, fully human, yet the divine son of God.

How to read the Gospel? At one sitting without stopping on the way, and by repeating the process " until the central figure haunts us like a melody," confronting us. Try reading the Gospel in a modern translation by Moffatt, Weymouth, Goodspeed, or

Phillips. Ask relevant questions: What did it mean to the writer? What was the situation that may have produced it? What does it mean to me today? What word of God reaches me through these words? What must I do because of it?

I. *Mark's story of Jesus.* Early tradition declares the author to have been John Mark, a native of Jerusalem and a son of a Christian woman whose house became the rendezvous of Christian leaders after Pentecost (Acts 12: 12). See Mark 14: 51 for a thinly disguised autobiographical reference. Mark accompanied Paul and Barnabas on his first missionary tour (Acts 13: 5, 13). Mark deserted them and forfeited Paul's friendship, but within a decade he shared Paul's imprisonment in Rome (Col. 4: 10-12; Philemon 24; II Tim. 4: 11). Mark's is also the story told by Simon Peter. Behind this Gospel is a sailor's logbook, the recollections of Peter. See the tender reference in the epistle bearing the big fisherman's name, " my son Mark." The early, reliable tradition of Papias, dating to the first half of the second century, affirms that Mark acted as Peter's interpreter when he preached, and later used the materials so received when he composed his Gospel.

II. *Main divisions of the " log."* (1) Prologue (Mark 1: 1-13). Note the terse and dramatic beginning, devoid of any reference to the birth or childhood of Jesus. (2) First main section (Mark 1: 14 to 8: 38). After John the Baptizer's arrest, Jesus begins his ministry. A decisive hour of history has struck; God's reign begins. Let men " turn again " to God and believe the good news. Christ teaches his followers. Enemies' hostility grows. Peter makes his great confession of faith. (3) Second main section (Mark 9: 1 to 16: 8). Here is the story of Jesus to the crucifixion, and its astonishing sequel, " He is risen." (4) The epilogue (Mark 16: 9-20). Mark's original Gospel ends at v. 8. Was it torn off accidentally? What we have is by a later hand.

III. *Mark's portrait of Christ.* (1) Jesus is completely human, experiences fatigue, discouragement, and — on the cross — even a sense of forsakenness by God. (2) Yet Christ emerges clearly, unmistakably as the Son of God. (3) Jesus is shown in the context of controversy and of increasing tension and opposition to him and to his mission. (4) Christ's "martyrdom" is given unusual prominence. More than one third of the entire narrative is devoted to his trial, death, and resurrection. Yet this death is much more than martyrdom; it is redemptive sacrifice of cosmic significance, which, with his resurrection, affects man's relationship with God.

IV. *Mark's appeal for the hearer.* This Gospel, like the other three, is written "that you may believe that Jesus is the Christ, the Son of God, and that believing you may have life in his name" (John 20: 31). Do you accept this life? If so, then you must: (1) respond with loving trust and obedience, whatever the cost; (2) give absolute loyalty to the fellowship of the church, through which alone the message comes down to us, and through which Christ continues his redemptive mission work today; and (3) accept responsibility to proclaim the gospel everywhere, since Christ lived and died and conquered death for all men.

"On Eagles' Wings"

I bore you on eagles' wings and brought you to myself.

EXODUS 19: 4.

They who wait for the Lord shall renew their strength, they shall mount up with wings like eagles.

ISAIAH 40: 31.

When the Jewish pilgrims reached the Sinai wilderness and encamped before the mountain, Moses had an interview with the Eternal. He received a directive for his people, and it included a reminder that God had sustained them as "on eagles' wings" and brought them to himself.

As we read and appreciate the Fourth Gospel, we feel that God could say this of the author. Like the wise and trusting soul of whom Isaiah wrote, the Gospel writer had waited upon the Lord of life and glory until wings were given his mind and spirit. Then he soared into heavenly places of spiritual insight, returning to inspire and illumine earth-born mortals with his sublime book.

Saint John, said a famous scholar, loves a circling flight, like his symbol, the eagle. There is in this Gospel a hovering and a brooding over the truth men most need to know.

> " John mounts on eagles' wings, and, far above,
> Broods on the utmost meaning of God's Love
> in Christ. Here is the Son of God disclosed,
> Who from the first Eternity reposed
> In God, with God, as God, and was made Man
> For our salvation, in God's ageless plan.
> This is the Gospel of God's Heart made Bread
> and Wine to feed and vivify the dead."
>
> —*A. Boyd Scott*

Who was the author? Who was this Saint John who gave us the Gospel of the altitudes? Tradition answers, John the apostle. Certainly the authority of the apostle John lies behind this writing. The actual form and penmanship may have come from another hand. So the Gospel may be described as the " Gospel of John the Elder according to John the son of Zebedee " (A. M. Hunter).

I. *Clues to understanding the Gospel According to Saint John.*

1. This Gospel is different from the other Gospels. It is different in the selection of incidents from Christ's life, in the scene of his ministry, in the form and substance of his teaching, in the chronology or time sequence of events, and in what it omits: no account of birth, baptism, temptations, the Last Supper, Gethsemane, or ascension. No word is found here of the healing of people possessed by demons, and there are no parables. It is different in the stories told about Jesus: his talks with Nicodemus and with the woman at Jacob's well; the raising of Lazarus from the dead; the washing of the disciples' feet on the last night before the crucifixion; the resurrection appearances, first to Mary Magdalene in the garden, then to doubting Thomas in the upper room, and, last of all, to seven disciples by the lake in the gray of a Galilean dawn.

2. John had special knowledge. If he differs from the other

three Gospels, it is not because he is ignorant. He tells us much that the other Gospels did not say (see John 2: 1-11; 3: 1-15; chs. 4; 11; 13: 1-17), including his teaching about the Holy Spirit, the Comforter (chs. 14 to 17).

Further evidence of his specialized knowledge is found in his intimate and detailed knowledge of the geography and history of Palestine and Jerusalem.

3. John wrote because, in his time, the church was challenged by the Gentile world. Christianity had to be restated for people with a Greek background who did not wish to make a detour through Judaism. So John chose the Greek conception of the Logos (word, reason). It was in this category of the mind of God that John thought of Jesus.

4. The church was also challenged by the rise of heresy within it. Seventy years had passed since the crucifixion. Jewish Christians tended to give too high a place to John the Baptist. So this Gospel carefully points out that John is not the true light (ch. 1: 8).

Also widespread was a heresy called Gnosticism. Its basic doctrine was that matter is essentially evil and spirit is essentially good. Gnostics argued that since that is so, God cannot touch matter; therefore, he did not create the world. Emanations God launched created the world! They concluded that the creator god was different from, ignorant of, and hostile to the real God. That is why John ringingly declares that "all things were made through him" (v. 3) and that "God so loved the world" (ch. 3: 16).

Some of the Gnostics held that Jesus was one of the emanations that proceeded from God, and so not in any real sense divine. He was only a sort of demigod. Others held that Jesus had no real body. Because a body is matter, Jesus to them was a phantom. They never could have said, "The Word became flesh." This particular heresy is known as Docetism from a Greek word meaning "to seem." To them, Jesus only seemed to be a man. So these Gnostic beliefs destroyed for their adherents the real deity and the real manhood of Jesus.

John seeks to correct both these heresies. He stresses the real manhood of Jesus. He was angry (John 2:15), physically tired (ch. 4:6), hungered (ch. 4:31), and he sympathized with the fear-ridden and hungry (ch. 6:5, 20). He knew grief and wept real tears (ch. 11:33, 35, 38). He knew terrible thirst (ch. 19:28). Jesus is truly human in this portrait.

This Gospel stressed the deity and godhead of Jesus. He is pre-existent (chs. 8:58; 17:5; 6:33-38). He knows more than any ordinary man could (chs. 4:16-17; 5:6; 6:6; 6:61-64; 11:14). He acted on his own initiative. He laid down his life voluntarily (chs. 10:18; 19:11).

5. In John's Gospel the discourses of Jesus are extended, and are concerned almost entirely with the great themes of life: light, love, trust, and Christ's relationships with the Father.

6. Symbolism and allegory run throughout the work. The numbers three and seven are frequent. Note the seven "signs," or miracles, from which arise significant teachings concerning Christ and his work.

II. *Purpose*. John himself sums it up: "That you may believe that Jesus is the Christ, the Son of God, and that believing you may have life in his name" (ch. 20:31).

III. *Value of John's Gospel*.

1. This is the spiritual Gospel. In the early third century, Clement of Alexandria said: "Last of all, John, perceiving that what had reference to the bodily things of Jesus' ministry had been sufficiently related, and encouraged by his friends, and inspired by the Holy Spirit, wrote a spiritual Gospel."

2. He sums up the message of the Gospel for all time in one great, golden sentence: "God so loved the world, that he gave his only begotten Son, that whosoever believeth in him should not perish, but have everlasting life" (ch. 3:16).

3. Here is the most adequate portrait of Jesus for Christians.

a. Jesus Christ is the symbol of God's eternal life. If you see him, you see the Father.

b. Christ is the decisive factor in history, because he is the decisive personality. He is the Living Bread, the Light of the World, the Door, the Good Shepherd, the Resurrection and the Life, the Way and the Truth, the Vine. He is the soul's inexhaustible resource.

c. He is the supernatural Redeemer, the Lord of Glory. Christ gives eternal life to anyone who is "oriented toward God in Jesus Christ."

d. Christ's Second Coming to earth is spiritual. "I will come to you" — in the Holy Spirit.

e. He is the key to the riddle of the universe, the Life and Light of our souls.

4. This book influences the faith and life of more Christians than any other book in the Bible. Simple souls and learned scholars alike have brooded over it — and meditate on it today — finding its insights and words unique and enriching. Its final word is, "Only those who love will ever understand."

Christian Manifesto by a Five-Star General

Nineteen hundred years ago the moral and spiritual conflict for the soul of man and society broke out into open warfare in a province of the Roman Empire. This holy war continues, and will continue until history's end. But the ultimate result was determined by the mighty acts of God in the life, death, and resurrection of Jesus Christ. In the four Gospels and in The Acts, we have the historical narrative of the decisive campaign. But to understand more fully the significance of the issues and our relation to them, we require the official papers of the field commanders, the dispatches and reports of Christ's ablest generals. These we possess in the epistles, or letters, of our New Testament. Of twenty-seven New Testament books, twenty-one are letters from the first Christian army leaders. Christ's "five-star generals" were the apostles. The ablest strategist, interpreter, and thinker was the apostle Paul.

I. *Career and character of Paul.* From his "aide-de-camp," Luke, writing in the book of The Acts, and from Paul's letters we learn the main facts. Here a brief recital of the main facts about Paul can be given, concluding with some such tribute as: During his thirty-two years as a soldier of the cross, he fought inwardly against a sore physical disability. He suffered almost every kind of adverse experience. Through blood, sweat, toil and tears, he endured with undaunted courage because his living Lord stood by him. Never very long in one place, he remained for a year or two in the great cities of his world — Antioch, Corinth, Ephesus, Caesarea, and Rome. He died a martyr's death about A.D. 67.

1. Appearance. No authentic portrait has survived. From The Acts of Paul and Thekla, which never received apostolic acceptance, we may have a first-century description: "A man of moderate stature, with curly hair and scanty; crooked legs; blue eyes, and large, knit eyebrows; long nose; and he was full of grace and pity of the Lord, sometimes having the appearance of a man, but sometimes looking like an angel."

2. His writings. He rarely had leisure to write a book. Never discharged from active duty, he wrote much, but what he wrote resembled dispatches and army orders and the answering of reports from other parts of the field. Always he had what he called the pressing business of each day, "the care of all the churches" (II Cor. 11:28). Thirteen of the twenty-one New Testament letters are attributed to Paul, and ten seem to be by him. One exception to the kind of letters described above is the epistle to the Romans. This is more than a letter "written on the run."

II. *Our "book of the month" — Romans.* This book is less a letter than it is a comprehensive manifesto — a public declaration and platform, a statement of aims, and an interpretation of actions. It is a manifesto of Paul's gospel in various relations. If Paul were to write today, he might entitle it "Why I Believe" or "The Gospel According to Paul." The influence of Romans has been profound. Rediscovery of its truth has inspired many of the spiritual awakenings and advances of the church. Augustine, Luther, Wesley, and, in our own time, Karl Barth, the influential

Swiss theologian, have found the truth as it is in Christ, coming alive through their study of Romans.

1. Date and place. It was written in Corinth about A.D. 58, seven or eight years before our earliest Gospel, Mark. No one knows who founded the church in Rome. The church must have been large; less than a decade after Paul wrote to this church, Christians there were described by Tacitus as "an immense multitude," representing a public danger. Paul had friends in Rome, and he longed to visit the city. After conducting his own every member canvass for funds for the Jerusalem saints, he planned to go to Rome and even to Spain (Rom. 15:24). So he called for his secretary, Tertius (ch. 16:22), and dictated a letter "to all God's beloved in Rome, who are called to be saints."

2. The letter itself. Professor A. M. Hunter admits that Romans is "heavy going." But Paul was handling tremendous themes — considering God and the world and life and death in the light of the new fact of Christ. Many of his figures of speech and thought forms are unfamiliar, and probably uncongenial to us. One of the best ways to understand the letter is to read it in a translation by Moffatt, Goodspeed, or Phillips, and with the help of a recent commentary. The theme of Romans may be tersely stated as "salvation, its root and fruit."

3. Outline. Prologue (ch. 1:1-15); salvation, its root (chs. 1:16 to 8:39); philosophy of history (chs. 9 to 11); salvation, its fruit (chs. 12:1 to 15:13); epilogue (chs. 15:14 to 16:25). The key or central truth is contained in ch. 1:16-17.

4. What should we do because of it? We should live ourselves into its dynamic truth. Coleridge pronounced it "the most profound work ever written." Calvin said it "opened the door to all the treasures in the Scriptures." Luther called it the "chief book of the New Testament and the purest Gospel." In this manifesto we have the answer to the question, "What is Christianity?" by one of the strongest thinkers of the church. The word of God it contains still has power to reach and change and energize you and me.

II

CHRISTMASTIDE

Season of the Nativity

CHRISTMAS

A Christmas Emphasis

Christmas means crowds, children, carols, candy, kindness, for most of us in the Western Hemisphere. For Christians, it should mean Christ. Preachers may help to rescue Christmas from the secularization that has all but smothered it beneath the tinsel which sentimentalists and salesmen heap upon it. But we would not forgo the sentiment which "gentles" our spirits. Keeping Christmas in the heart, as children do, prepares us for Him who came "a little baby thing" to confound the wisdom that is not wise. While pedantic theological dissertations on the incarnation are out of place in this season, our messages must transmit the central truth that the festival celebrates: God "has visited and redeemed his people" (Luke 1:68), and therefore we rejoice.

Does anyone need to be convinced that this is an imperative emphasis? Pressures of our crowd culture tend to push the divine significance of Christ's birth almost out of sight. Not a few genial and philanthropic pagans are surprised, even discomfited, by this fact. They respond as did the woman in the story of the community Christmas concert. This public-spirited and "emancipated" modern requested a minister to suggest suitable carols for the occasion. When she scanned his selection, she exclaimed in dismay, "But they're all so distressingly theological!" To which the only true answer is, "That's the way it is."

Consider a few New Testament references: "In these last days he has spoken to us by a Son, whom he appointed the heir of all things, through whom also he created the world" (Heb.

1:2). "'And his name shall be called Emmanuel' (which means, God with us)" (Matt. 1:23). "And he will reign . . . and of his kingdom there will be no end" (Luke 1:33). "The Word became flesh and dwelt among us, full of grace and truth; we have beheld his glory, glory as of the only Son from the Father. . . . And from his fulness have we all received, grace upon grace" (John 1:14, 16). Christmas untheological? We might as well ask that life should be unbiological! Let one sermon this Christmastide proclaim the deep truth of God's unique self-disclosure and self-giving in the Child "laid on the doorstep of the world."

The Expression of God

Christmas and conflict, incarnation and insurrection, revelation and revolution — to bracket such mutually exclusive terms sounds like a kind of theologian's game of "Scrabble." Certainly most church members and citizens generally do not think of Christmas and the fact it celebrates in such paradoxical fashion. When we see how Christmas has been captured and exploited by business, we have moments when we wonder whether the festival suggests anything but frenzied shopping, frantic revels, over-eating and excessive drinking. Of course, gifts in the name of Love have their place, and who would prohibit innocent revels in this happy season of the year? If the religious significance of Christmas could be banished, one suspects that humanitarians would compel retention of some such celebration as Christmas inspires. In a world like this there must be a lyrical interlude in the *miserere* of life.

But Christmas' profound meaning can be sentimentalized out of existence. Its transforming truth can be pushed to the dim horizon of men's thoughts. Christ's messengers must rescue Christmas from its secularized champions! One way to do it is to indicate how the new divine energy that entered the world in the baby Jesus divided and divides men and nations. Remember what Simeon said to Mary, the child's mother: "This child is destined to make many fall and many rise in Israel and to set up a standard which many will attack — for he will expose the secret thoughts of many hearts" (Luke 2: 34-35, Phillips). Does not the subsequent story of that Child, as recorded in the New Testament and in nineteen centuries of history, fulfill that prophecy?

As for revolution — radical change of direction and motive and life — has there been any more dynamic factor in creating it than the One who came "a little baby thing" at Bethlehem? Again and again, God in Christ has turned aside the stream of history and lifted empires off their hinges. And it all began when, as J. B. Phillips paraphrases John 1: 14, "the Expression of God became a human being and lived among us."

The Gospel of Christmas

I. *The gospel of Christmas: release from fear.* "Fear not: for, behold, I bring you good tidings of great joy" (Luke 2: 10). "Do not be afraid! Listen, I bring you glorious news of great joy which is for every man" (Phillips).

First and most of all, the "glorious news" of Christmas is for the fearful. Who has not known, or does not know, fear? Adam confessed, "I was afraid," and every descendant of Adam can say the same. Psychologists chart human fears from A to Z — from acrophobia, fear of heights, to zoophobia, fear of animals. Think of prevalent fears today. William James said the fear of poverty is the American's idea of hell. What about "nucleomitophobia" — a Baltimore physician's word for fear of atomic war?

What can be done about fears? Practical wisdom suggests steps in conquest of these foes of our health and usefulness. Face them for what they are. Some of them keep us from folly and sickness, accidents and death. Most of them are blackmailers, and the more we yield to them the more we have to yield! Action helps. Shake that bush supposed to be a bear! If the engine of your mind and imagination is racing, throw in the clutch. But the real cure is deeper. "The real victorv over fear is not in anything we can do, or even in anything a minister or psychologist can do for us, but in some sign given by the universe that these deep yearnings [for health, for companionship, for peace] of which our fears are but the broken sign, are known and satisfied." So wrote an expert in the field of psychotherapy. Christmas is the proof that such a sign has been given. If Christ came as we know he did, if Christ is what faith has found him to be, there is no need to worry. Among the first words concerning Jesus Christ are these: "Fear not!" Among the last words ascribed to the glorified Lord are these: "Fear not; I am the first and the last: I am he that liveth . . . and, behold, I am alive for evermore . . . ; and have the keys of hell and of death" (Rev. 1:17-18).

Christmas' deep meaning is that at the center of this mysterious life there lives and reigns a God like Christ, a God who in Christ cares for the least and littlest of us. "God became in Christ like us in order that we might become like him," said Clement of Alexandria in the morning years of the church. This love and power we can experience as we respond to Him with loving trust and obedience. Perfect love is the antidote for fear. Such love he freely gives; and such love, toward God and our fellow humans, he creates in us. God's love for us, made known uniquely in Christ, and our answering love for him cast out fear.

II. *The gospel of Christmas: joy*. Joy, or at least happiness, is recognized as something we ought to possess. Much of our world may be in chaos, many hearts failing for fear of what tomorrow may bring, but this month the most frequently heard greeting is "Merry Christmas!" Christians ought to be joyous as they keep Christmas. "I bring you good news of a great joy that is to be felt by all the people," said the Christmas angel to the shepherds. (Luke 2:10.) Even when diluted by sentimentalism and secularism, Christmas makes people sing. Atheism has no jubilant anthems, nor has skepticism its lilting carols. Christmas is truly the joyous mystery.

What are the elements of joy in the good news of Christmas? You could begin by citing obvious elemental facts such as the smile of a baby and the laughter of children. You would move on to the fact that many celebrants seem to forget: the Baby grew up. The Man Christ Jesus blazed the trail into life that has joy at its center. In a world as tragic and evil as this, he lived and came victor over personal and impersonal forces ranged against him. He is the incarnation of our sublimest hopes. He came and taught that his joy might be in us.

Yet although his life, his teachings, his spirit, might awaken hope within us and the joy that hope brings, this hope would remain unfulfilled, even a mockery, if Jesus stood alone, unrelated to the nature of things.

Hence, the deepest joy of Christmas issues from the central fact of faith: in the life begun in a manger, continued throughout manhood, and "ended" on a cross, God himself acted uniquely and redemptively. God "has visited and redeemed his people" in Jesus Christ. Christmas marks the divine intrusion. Christmas as a memory or a wistful hope can never heal our deepest hurts; but Christmas as a reproducible spiritual experience, the visitation of our souls by God himself, heals, empowers, and saves. He made us for himself. He is here. Close to our need is his helping. The lost can be found, the dead can be restored to life. This is the joy of Christmas.

III. *The gospel of Christmas: peace.* "And in a flash there appeared with the angel a vast host of the armies of Heaven, praising God, saying, 'Glory to God in the highest Heaven! Peace upon earth to men whom He loves!'" (Luke 2: 13-14, Phillips.)

Sounding the climacteric note in the angels' song, remind your hearers of what they know, or should know.

1. Most people everywhere want peace. Is such desire doomed to disappointment? Toynbee is sure that nothing superhuman or suprahistorical makes our extinction in war inevitable. A wide area exists in which human will can operate to change the course of history. In politics, a constitutional, co-operative system of international law and order can be established — however im-

perfect. In economics, working compromises between free enterprise and "socialism" may be worked out. In the life of the spirit, we may "put the secular superstructure back on to religious foundations." He adds that of the three tasks, the religious one is, of course, in the long run, most important. Christianity is the supreme relevancy. God himself is the author of peace, and he has taken the initiative. To his human family he has given the tremendous gift of choice: freedom to move toward reasonable harmony or toward chaos. Christmas is the prophecy and promise of peace.

2. It follows that peace in the world depends upon the individuals in community who have God's peace within. Religious experience may not be a substitute for sound economic, social, and political solutions of global difficulties; but it is prerequisite to and assurance of such solutions. Said the late Rabbi Joshua Liebman, "When men are at peace within themselves, the explosive emotions that now torment them will die away."

3. This is where Christ comes in! His birth was preceded by the promise of peace to men whom God loves. His life was dedicated to the creation of peace with God and peace with one another. "He is our peace," declares the New Testament. His sacrificial death which overcame the enmity which causes war and which ended the alienation of man from himself, from his fellows, and from God, was preceded by his legacy: "My peace I give to you."

Christ's glorious good news is that in him we may have peace, and through him we may create conditions of peace among men. "Therefore being justified by faith, we have peace with God through our Lord Jesus Christ" (Rom. 5:1). You would then clearly point to the steps whereby Christ's peace can be experienced. And Christmas would see at least a few accepting the Holy Spirit's inexhaustible resource to be peacemakers. They would know that the Lord of peace himself came to give them "peace always by all means."

Do You Know This Christmas Hymn?

What pastor has not heard requests for "the good old Christmas hymns" or for familiar carols? Oldest and most glorious is the great hymn in Luke 1:46-55. E. Stanley Jones said, "The Magnificat is the most revolutionary document in the world." It speaks of three revolutions of God.

I. *The moral revolution.* Christianity aims at killing human pride. "He scatters the proud in the plans of their hearts." Christ in a soul shames the pride out of him. O. Henry tells the story of the village boy who sat beside a lovely girl in school. She returned his affection. Later, he moved to a city and into the city's basest ways. Now a pickpocket, he snatched an old lady's wallet and almost immediately saw his boyhood sweetheart coming down the street. Still sweet with the radiance of goodness, she unconsciously rebuked the evil in him. Leaning his burning head against a lamppost he said, "God, I wish I could die." He saw himself. Christ does this for a person. And such self-seeing strikes a deadly blow at pride.

II. *The social revolution.* "He casts down the mighty — he exalts the humble." The world's classifications, labels, and prestige mean nothing in the real society of Christ. Since Christ came, we no longer can speak contemptuously or patronizingly of the "common" man.

III. *The economic revolution.* Marxists and other deluded extremists may laugh at such a suggestion. But the steady, if slow, transformation of the world's economic life from scarcity and exploitation to abundance and increasing mutual aid and equitable distribution of goods can be seen. "He has filled those who are hungry, . . . those who are rich he has sent empty away." Wrote William Barclay: "A Christian society is a society where no man dares to have too much while others have too little, where every man must get only to give away."

The Simplicity of Christmas

Here follows a meditation that seems to ignore the complexities and theological subtleties inherent in much discussion of the incarnation and related doctrines. It was given as a radio talk on Christmas Eve. Sunday school teachers and their pupils had arranged a little Nativity scene in a room adjoining the sanctuary.

Not far from where I stand to speak to you is a Christmas crèche, a miniature of the Bethlehem stable on that night of nights when "the Hope of all the world was born." Grouped round the crib are figures of angels, shepherds, and kings, with drowsy cattle near. On fragrant hay in a manger lies the Child, tended by his mother. Understanding Joseph stands in the shadow of an angel's wing. Above the thatched roof a blue star gleams. To this Nativity tableau come many pilgrims, young and old.

Not long ago I stood beside a very young lady whose eyes danced with delight as she examined every minute detail of the crèche. "Those are the Wise Men, you know, and that's one of their camels outside the door. Look at that sleepy donkey and that sweet little lamb. Those are shepherds. And the mother, Mary—isn't her blue cloak lovely? And Joseph—he looks like a carpenter, doesn't he? And look at the dear baby Jesus. Isn't he sweet and chubby?" Not wishing to appear woefully ignorant, I added my word: "Yes, and there's the star too, up there above the roof. Do you suppose the starlight shines into the stable?" My little Christmas guide pointed to chinks in the roof: "Of course it does. That's why it's so lovely and bright inside. You can't see how the light comes in unless you get down and look up!"

"You can't see how the light comes in unless you get down and look up!"

It's just as simple as that! Kneel down, look up, and through!

> "The entrance to His place of birth
> Was by a little door,

So humble all might find him there,
The wise, the rich, the poor.

"A little door, where cows had passed,
Opened to a King!
The shepherds and the Wise Men bent
To see so fair a thing.

"Somewhere upon a far-off hill
At Christmas time,
At Christmas time,
A little door creaks open still —
It opens still."

Do you suppose that we could bend low enough in humility and simple wonder to pass through that door "to see so fair a thing"? If we could leave outside for a brief time our sophistication and cleverness and become as little children, we should find a new glory in Christmas and in life itself. It's the simplicity of Christmas that we must recover. A saint of our time said: "It begins with a carol, sweet clean music; with shepherds, symbols of simplicity; and if there are wise men in the picture, they are certainly not college dons!" That simple, human note remains through the whole story, even to the cross. And only simple souls grasp the deep meaning of it, and enter into the Kingdom of joy and peace.

"Simple" — well, you and I do not relish the adjective applied to us. We think of "simpleton," and we'd much rather be called shrewd! But "simple" once meant straightforward, natural, crystal-clear. When an intellectual giant named Paul muses on the Man Christ Jesus, the word "simplicity" drops from his pen: "the simplicity that is in Christ," the "simplicity" that is toward Christ. Nothing complicated about it, says the apostle. But you must get down and look up to see the light shining through.

"Gentle Jesus, meek and mild,
Look upon a little child;
Pity my simplicity,
Suffer me to come to thee."

Of course, he is much more than " meek and mild," this " strong Son of God, immortal love," and he wields a terrible swift sword against all that desecrates human life. But we must begin with the A B C's of our faith, and that means coming simply. We're not yet in the " upper forms " of Christ's school.

The liberating truth of Christianity is simple. One philosopher spoke of it as absurd, it was so simple! That the eternal Creator-Spirit of the universe should embody himself in the human personality of a Jewish maiden's wee lad! The mighty God " contracted to a span." It's not simple in the sense of explaining the mystery of it. Simplicity and mystery are not incompatibles. The incarnation is profound mystery. But in essence it's simple, so that simple folk like you and me could see the light of God shining through " that one Face." That is why on Christmas Day we let loose the " dear humanities," when we see again that, to be great, life must be simple; when we begin to find God human and intimate enough for our need.

When God wanted to assure us of his goodness, he turned the commonplace into a miracle of divine love. He sent, not celestial legions to coerce our obedience, but a babe to make a woman cry. Just as simple as that — and as divine! If we are wise, we bend our knees before the splendor of God, and see with the eyes of a child that God enters man's life by lowly doors. " You get down and look up! " said my little friend.

" To be Himself a star most bright
To bring the Wise Men to his sight,
To be himself a voice most sweet
To call the shepherds to his feet,
To be a child — it was his will
That folk like us might find him still."

— *John Erskine*

Do you turn from the ominous headlines to protest hotly, " Christianity's just too simple for a world as complicated and evil as this "? Life *is* complicated, and we must not oversimplify its problems. Nevertheless, the truth that makes us free is simple.

It marches down the Bethlehem road through cities of dreadful night, sounding solving words "that constrain us to rest and unanxious trust, that call us into the open to go to school" to a Master who speaks simply of losing one's life in service to others. The very simplicity of the Way and the Truth perplexes the learned, annoys the sophisticated, and makes the stupid dismiss it all as childish. You come to the end and find yourself standing on a hill, before a cross that was simple enough, two beams and some nails and a quivering body on it — and you find yourself bending down and looking up as the Light shines through. The story that has changed the world, and will change it, began with a simple cry from a crib and a heart-tearing cry from a cross.

"O stricken world, look up and see;
The God who died upon a tree
Is born a laughing Babe again
To bring new hope to weary men.

"Here is a legend never old —
Neither the dark nor the bitter cold
Can stay his coming once a year
To heal the sick and cast out fear.

"Bring him your hunger, bring your thirst;
The blind and crippled shall be first;
The most dejected and forlorn
Shall lie upon his breast this morn."

I begin to see now, as I hope you do, that I must kneel down before that divine Child and look up if I am to glimpse "the light of the knowledge of the glory of God in the face of Jesus Christ." Then I shall follow him in as simple trust and obedience as I can summon.

Let's Rescue Christmas!

Now when they had departed, behold, an angel of the Lord appeared to Joseph in a dream and said, "Rise, take the child and his mother, and flee to Egypt, and remain there till I tell you; for Herod is about to search for the child, to destroy him."

MATTHEW 2:13.

Herod sought to destroy all that made the first Christmas. Brutal forces confronted the starshine on a newly born child. Brutal and consenting forces confront Christmas on this anniversary of the divine event. General William Booth's wife asked her oldest daughter, " Kate, why is it that God can't keep a thing pure for more than a generation? " We ask that question about Christmas. Further, we ask, how did the " impurity " take over? What can we do to rescue Christmas from the stained hands which degrade it? You could voice a plea for a crusade to rescue Christmas in various ways. Here's one bare outline:

1. Let's rescue Christmas from the greedy, the selfish, and the thoughtless.

2. Let's rescue Christmas from the arrogant and intolerant who despise the race from which — humanly — Christmas came, and from all others who would exclude any of God's children from the feast he has prepared.

3. Let's rescue Christmas from the cynic and the skeptic, who insist that the Christmas message of God's incarnation in Jesus Christ is too good to be true.

4. And let's save Christmas from being ruined by childishness and give it back to the childlike of heart. Shortly before his death, Lloyd C. Douglas wrote a message entitled " Advent for Adults." In it he said: " This year we've got to get Christmas out of the cradle. We've got some machinery in motion, this time, that no baby can operate." Childishness runs to the cradle, but bypasses Galilee and Calvary and Olivet. Childlikeness enters the Kingdom of Heaven. Trust, awe, wonder, and love are the passports into the heavenly country.

Christmas to the Rescue

And the Lord said, I have surely seen the affliction of my people . . . and have heard their cry . . . ; for I know their sorrows; and I am come down to deliver them out of the hand of the Egyptians, and to bring them up out of that land unto a good land.

EXODUS 3:7-8.

The "incredible star" of Christmas hovers near the burning bush in the desert, where Moses heard God say, "I am come down to deliver." Let your people take a quick look at twentieth-century Egyptians, today's slave drivers. From what tyrants does the Christ of Christmas rescue us?

I. *From "the night view of history."* God's invasion of the world in Jesus discloses his purpose, gives meaning to the human drama, and meaning to our struggle. The God who came at Christmas rescues us from enslavement to the impersonal, delivers us from the oppressive sense of our helplessness in face of titanic forces loose in the world. Love divine and Power that men call weakness has allied himself to us as we fight against "anarchs of the night." One with him is a majority.

II. *Christmas — Christ — rescues us from fear of the dark* — the dark caused by our failures, by the blackout of despair, by the fact of death. The light of Christmas, as well as of Calvary and of Easter, is the light of God's forgiveness, his available transforming love, his eternal companionship. "To you is born . . . a Savior, . . . Christ the Lord"! God has heard, he has seen our plight, he knows our need, he is come. Salvation is created in the midst of all the earth. Alleluia!

Christmas Journeys

What about a sermon on "Christmas Journeys"? Five are mentioned in the two Gospels that alone record the Nativity. Look at Luke 1:39-56; 2:4-5; 2:16; Matt. 2:1, 11, 12; 21:37.

1. Let the first represent a journey to an understanding friend.

2. The second is the journey to Bethlehem. To make this trek is to travel the path of preparation.

3. To travel with the shepherds is to travel the trail of expectation.

> " Not where the wheeling systems darken,
> And our benumbed conceiving soars!
> The drift of pinions, would we harken,
> Beats at our own clay-shuttered doors.
>
> " The angels keep their ancient places;
> Turn but a stone and start a wing!
> 'Tis ye, 'tis your estranged faces,
> That miss the many-splendored thing."
> —*Francis Thompson*

4. The journey of the Magi may speak of the way of worship. To kneel in adoring awe before the Infinite in a little naked mite is to join the wisest Christmas pilgrims.

Reflections on the journey after the first Christmas " by night . . . to Egypt " may be reserved for a Sunday after Christmas Day. This dramatizes the grim fact that this is the kind of world in which the innocent, and God himself, may be a displaced person, an exile, a refugee. Also, that God's providence " moves in a mysterious way his wonders to perform."

5. This is the greatest of all journeys — that made by God himself! God so loved the world that he journeyed into time, into human life, choosing " the weak things of the world to confound the . . . mighty." They " shall call his name Immanuel," said the prophet — " God with us," God in a human personality. This is the divine invasion; here is how our inhumanity may be redeemed, our humanity transfigured.

Sang a contemporary, James Allen Kestle:

> " Somehow God weaves the strangest thing
> Into a pattern fair;
> He took an angel song, a star,
> A Hebrew peasant pair,
> Some shepherds on Judean hills
> And unknown Wise Men three,

A stable cold and dark and damp,
A manger 'neath an inn —
And now
  A weary world kneels hopefully
Before the Babe of Bethlehem."

Christmas Mail

Three texts ask for attention: "The posts went with the letters" (II Chron. 30: 6). Our old friend the postman is mentioned in the Bible! And he deserves recognition. "Is there any word from the Lord?" (Jer. 37: 17). To Jeremiah's question comes the divine answer: "The Word became flesh and dwelt among us," in John's glorious prologue to the Fourth Gospel. Thank God, our faith began not as an idea or a philosophy, but as a Nativity. Our Lord Jesus Christ was God's superlative, dynamic word to us, and for us.

"Light from a Half-shut Stable Door"

The title is borrowed from a line in a poem by Alfred Domett. Only in that light can we see the meaning of Christmas, of childhood, of ourselves, of the conflict between the Herods and the Savior, of the nature and purpose of God himself. (See Luke 2: 32.)

The Christmas Dynasty

There may be a sermon for you in the thought of the Christmas "dynasty." You might lift out of its context (Paul's exposition of predestination) words in Rom. 8: 29: "That he might be the firstborn among many brethren." Dr. Moffatt's version conveys the tremendous claim: "For he decreed of old that those whom he predestined should share the likeness of his Son — that he might be the first-born of a great brotherhood."

The Christ-child is the first of a royal line of which you and I are to be members! The first Christmas is "the progenitor of many spiritual birthdays." How do we enter into this heritage and take our rightful place in the " dynasty "? How do we " have the Spirit of Christ," without which we are " none of his "? Your experience, and your insight born of it, will help you to give the answers.

Home for Christmas

Janet Peebles was a fugitive, but she didn't need to be. How could we reach her with the news that would make all the difference? There was just a chance, her mother's letter said, that Janet would drop in at church on Sunday night. When she realized that her crime had been discovered, she had run away from the disgrace she was sure would wreck her family and ruin her reputation beyond repair. Someone had seen her board a train for a city some miles distant from her home town. She could lose herself in a strange city. No one would know her, and the only person she knew was the minister of one of the city churches. Nine years had passed since he had been her pastor, and now she had grown up. I was that minister, and her mother felt sure that she would come to hear me, but without disclosing her identity.

It was a pitiful letter that Mrs. Peebles had written. Her Scottish pride had to be trampled underfoot. A bed of nettles would have been easier to tread. Janet had stolen money belonging to the firm in which she had been a trusted accountant. Several hundred dollars, taken during a period of two years, had been successfully concealed until a company auditor uncovered clues that Janet knew would lead him straight to the damaging truth. Why had she done it? She knew so much better, said her mother, but she was evidently tired of scrimping along on a salary inadequate for the kind of clothes and good times a normal young woman wants. Better-paid jobs were not easy to find in the years preceding the war. As she entered the middle and later twenties, she wondered how she could get a good man if she didn't dress glamorously and if she were not seen in the right places? Of course, she meant to put the "borrowed" funds back, but her defalcation was discovered too soon. Of all times to be found out to be a common thief! Two weeks before Christmas and her gift to her dear ones — a prison sentence and intolerable shame!

"Janet's a good girl at heart. I'm not excusing her," the mother wrote. "No doubt we've all been at fault in not understanding her better and in not helping her more. But all that matters now is saving Janet from herself. I know she's sure it's hopeless. If she comes back, she'll be arrested and tried and sentenced, and she'd rather die than face that.

"But the wonderful thing is that she won't be. We've all forgiven her, and we love her more than ever. Her employer is willing to take her back and let her pay the money she took. He's even said he'll raise her wages, for he says he should have done it anyway. He says that Janet's been one of his most valued workers.

"But how can we get word to her that we all love her and really forgive her, that we will stand by her, and that it's not hopeless at all? I thought of putting a notice in the personal column of the papers, but she wouldn't see it. She's likely to be in your city now, and when Sunday comes, I have the strongest feeling she'll go to your church.

"You meant a lot to her when she was a girl in the church here. When Sunday night comes, she'll be lonely and afraid. I think she'll slip in to your service. Anyway, I am coming up myself, and I'll be at church and watch for her. Perhaps in your sermon or prayer you could say something that she'll take as a word to herself."

Was Janet's mother clairvoyant? Could this be a woman's intuition? The skeptic in me doubted it. But there was a slight possibility that Janet would come. She had always liked to attend church at the evening service. Guilt feelings, desperate insecurity, and loneliness would drive this child of Christian parents to God's house when others might seek relief in a movie or tavern. If she came, what could I say that would be indeed "a word to herself"?

How I worked on that service and sermon! Always a preacher

tries to speak to individuals in their actual needs. Now I had an object more definitely personal than I had dreamed. Yet what I said must not be too personal, too transparent in its intention. Suspicion must not be stimulated.

On the Sunday before Christmas it was not strange that I had chosen and announced the subject "Home for Christmas." City congregations have many persons who come from small towns and other places; they would want to spend Christmas in the old home. Starting with this normal desire, I would try to link it with the gospel invitation to return to Him who came at Christmas that all men might be at home. Janet's plight sharpened focus. I had a target for Sunday night. God helping me, I would not miss.

It was not so strange that I should have chosen that particular theme in the season. Preachers are wisely chary of ascribing providential direction to a choice of subject. Yet in the light of what happened during and after the service I am compelled to believe that I was guided even when I knew it not.

As I left the vestry for the processional to the chancel, I prayed that the Lord himself would speak through me with unwonted power, "for Jesus' sake"—yes, that first and last—but for Janet's sake too.

Christmas hymns and carols thrilled with new meaning, at least for the preacher. The glorious strains of "Adeste Fideles" brought the question, Would Janet hear the Lord himself inviting her—"O come . . . to Bethlehem"? Would Phillips Brooks's familiar words impel her tortured heart to pray:

"O holy Child of Bethlehem,
Descend to us, we pray;
Cast out our sin, and enter in;
Be born in us today."

In the pastoral prayer, I entreated the gracious and loving God to assure each troubled soul that in the divine love there is forgiveness and peace and power for a new beginning. As for the sermon, it broke all homiletical rules, and if any exegetical principles stood in the way, they were bypassed too. Our Lord's parable of the prodigal son was linked with the Nativity pictures of star-led pilgrims kneeling by the Baby " laid on the doorstep of the world." A forgotten saint's beatitude recurred as a kind of motif: " Blessed are the homesick, for they shall come at last to their Father's house." I told again the story Ralph Connor included in his novel *The Sky Pilot,* of the prodigal who, when life ebbed toward its close, found immeasurable comfort in hearing read the last letter received from his mother back in the Old Country: " And, oh, Davie, laddie, if ever your heart turns home again, remember that the doors are open and it's joy you'll bring with you to us all." God in Christ is saying that to every wanderer and exile who thinks longingly of home, hoping that we may think of him as the home of us all, and return at Christmas where all are welcome. The good news had to get through. Janet must receive the word of God she desperately needed to help her to face not only the worst but the best. She could be home for Christmas! Love bade her welcome.

Was Janet there? Yes. Her mother's guess was correct. I saw neither Janet nor her mother. Afterward an usher spoke of a touching little reunion between a gray-haired lady and a young woman. " Mother and daughter they must have been," he said. " After the others had gone, those two just stood there in the vestibule and held each other. I think they were crying a little — for joy, I guess. Funny what things go on in church, isn't it? "

A few days later a letter came, its envelope bearing the postmark I eagerly looked to see. It confirmed the usher's report. Mrs. Peebles had waited near the door after the service. As Janet left, the meeting took place that we three had conspired to make. We three? Do you doubt that there was Another who had the largest part in it? Janet was home for Christmas. The new year was going to be really new. Love never fails because God is love. Love's resourcefulness uses even " funny " things in church to fulfill his designs.

" To an open house in the evening,
Home shall men come,

To an older place than Eden
And a taller town than Rome.
To the end of the way of the wandering star,
To the things that cannot be and that are,
To the place where God was homeless,
And all men are at home."

— Gilbert Keith Chesterton

NEW YEAR SUNDAY

This Can Be the Best Year Yet

This sounds like a sales manager's pep talk to discouraged agents, or the diluted gospel favored by the superficial optimist. But it's the gospel! An Old Testament expression of it is found in the last part of the eleventh verse of Ezekiel's thirty-sixth chapter: " I . . . will do better unto you than at your beginnings." But the promise is for a purpose many secular optimists would prefer to " skip ": " and ye shall know that I am the Lord." Life " in Christ " is dynamic, never static; perfection is never attained once and for all. Whatever the heights reached " 'way back when," to the person and to the community that grow in the knowledge and love of the great God revealed in Christ, there is the promise of more yet. " I . . . will do better . . . than at your beginnings."

The Doors of the Years

I. *Please shut the door*. Who hasn't issued such requests or obeyed such instructions? If you speak at a Watch Night service and again on Sunday, you might do something with these familiar words. For the first, an uncommonly appealing word is that which Ezekiel heard the Lord speak to him: " This gate shall be shut, it shall not be opened, and no man shall enter in by it; because the Lord the God of Israel hath entered in by it, therefore it shall be shut " (Ezek. 44:2).

Shut the door on yesterday's failures, on yesterday's sins. Do it not only for your soul's health, but also for the sake of others, and for the sake of Christ's great cause. Has not God entered through that door and dealt bountifully with your past? Has he not forgiven you? Leave the past with him, and move with him into " the large room " of today and tomorrow.

II. *Please open the door.*

" Behold, I have set before you an open door, which no one is able to shut; I know that you have but little power, and yet you have kept my word and have not denied my name. . . . Behold, I stand at the door and knock; if any one hears my voice and opens the door, I will come in to him and eat with him, and he with me " (Rev. 3: 8, 20).

In one sense, as the glorified Christ, " the holy one " of the Revelation, assures John, the Lord of life and history opens and no one shall shut. All we can do is walk by trust and walk through. In another sense, as v. 20 hauntingly reminds us, the handle of the door is on our side. If we open the door, we shall entertain one who is both Guest and Host. To open life to Christ is to receive the key to life's meaning, to realize forgiveness, to be granted newness of life, to be given an assignment dangerous and thrilling with resources for its fulfillment.

Making the New Year Happy

Christ's joy (John 15: 11) is at once deeper and more abiding than what we commonly mean by happiness, and more of a gift than the result of pursuit. What are the essentials of true happiness? The late Dr. P. Carnegie Simpson wrote that the essentials consist of (1) someone to love, and (2) something to do. The great commandment and our Lord's definition of the supreme objective, " Seek ye first the kingdom of God," provide both.

Time on Your Hands

Then saith Jesus unto them, My time is not yet come: but your time is always ready. JOHN 7: 6.

Your time is always at hand. (MOFFATT.)

"The trouble with you is that you have too much time on your hands!" Did someone ever say that to you? But busy or idle, we have time on our hands. Here reference may be made to the speculations of J. W. Dunner in his book *An Experiment with Time*. If this book proves too obtuse or unavailable, your local library may have J. B. Priestley's book on an American visit, *Midnight on the Desert,* in which the British novelist confesses his fascination with this mysterious fact (see pp. 246 and 247). Argues Priestley, following Dunner and possibly Oupensky, the truth may be contained in our metaphors and ways of speaking of time as a movement. "Time, like an ever-rolling stream, Bears all its sons away." If time moves, what is the background against which it moves? Perhaps we travel along the path of time, a fourth dimensional track. The past has not been destroyed, but in all "its color and hum" yesterday and many days before are still active. The future? What we do may largely, actually, shape the future.

The New Testament insists that our time is "always ready," and on our hands is time past, present, future. The past can be changed — if God is brought into it. The present can be gloriously transformed as we redeem the time (Eph. 5:15) through our commitment and discipleship. The future may have victory assured in advance if we go in and possess the land of tomorrow in God's grace. To adapt familiar words of Tennyson's "Ulysses":

> "The long day wanes; the slow moon climbs; the deep
> Moans round with many voices. Come, my friends,
> 'Tis not too late to seek a newer world.
> Push off, and sitting well in order smite
> The sounding furrows; for [God's] . . . purpose holds
> To sail beyond the sunset, and the paths
> Of all the western stars."

Crystal Gazing

In I Sam. 28:11, Saul demands of the fortuneteller, when he traveled the road to Endor, "the craziest road of all," "Bring up

Samuel for me." Retell the dramatic story of the distraught king, pursued by fear, running to the medium and craving contact with the departed leader.

Many today seek deliverance in just such futile ways. "Stuck fast in yesterday," they would recover the old ways, now forever gone. To all such, and to all dismayed or frightened by the present or future, you may bring One who conquered death and who is our eternal Contemporary, the only leader we can follow with confidence. Is there "a ghost of a chance" that we can avert global terror, personal failure? Yes, if we give the Holy Spirit our trust and what a great thinker called "unconditional obedience."

Preview of the Future

For the land which you are entering to take possession of it is not like the land of Egypt, from which you have come, where you sowed . . . but the land which you are going over to possess is a land of hills and valleys, . . . a land which the Lord your God cares for; the eyes of the Lord your God are always upon it, from the beginning of the year to the end of the year.

DEUTERONOMY 11: 10-12.

I. *Time flies.* A prospective fountain pen purchaser wrote on the pad, "*Tempus fugit.*" The sales girl read what he had written and remarked helpfully, "Perhaps you'd like to try this one, Mr. Fugit!" Whatever fountain pen Mr. Fugit uses, time does fly. Its swift flight is brought home as last year moves into this year. Because we are human, we are curious about tomorrow. What will the terrain be like? What will befall us and our world in the year ahead? Here the ancient description of the new world into which the Israelites were moving furnishes spiritual clues for modern Christian pilgrims.

II. *Time's territory will be different* (v. 10). Change will meet us. New responsibilities and new possibilities for good or evil await us. It will be "a land of hills and valleys." Ascent and descent, aspiration and low levels, climbing and plodding will be on the route.

III. *A journey guided and guarded.* For the traveler who trusts the Lord of the encircling years, it will be a journey guided and guarded by infinite Wisdom and Love: "a land which the Lord your God cares for" (v. 12). We may fail and falter, retreat and weaken; he will never fail, nor will his divine providence grow weary: "The eyes of the Lord your God are always upon it [and, our Lord Jesus would add, upon you and all his children] from the beginning of the year to the end of the year."

That last verse would make an unforgettable text and theme for a New Year's message. Using such a word, you would be sure to stress God's watch-care, his unceasing concern regardless of our deserving, and that he whose eyes are on the sparrow watches his own children, employing love's strategy to bring the best out of them as well as to bring the best to them.

Are You Afraid of Tomorrow?

A glorious text is, "All things are yours; . . . things to come; all are yours; and ye are Christ's; and Christ is God's" (I Cor. 3: 21-23).

I. *The fearful future.* Describe the "shape of things to come" as it induces fear. Old and young alike take a dim and depressed view of the future. Bill Mauldin called his generation the "scared rabbit" generation. There is at least partial truth in the description. Few now expect happy consummations in life and history. Yet Christians should be men such as Thucydides hailed, "who dared beyond their strength, hazarded against their judgment, and in extremities were in excellent hope."

II. *Why should we be confident* concerning the unknown tomorrows? Because we belong to Christ, and through Christ to God, and this relationship makes "things to come" ours to use or endure or transform as God directs. Can we spell this out? Take the three affirmations a dauntless Christian leader in wartime Britain used to rally his own soul and the souls of his people. Everything seemed black and much was burning, but these three truths of faith gave the reinforcement and armed them with hope: (1) God reigns. (2) God cares. (3) God strives. Then from Scripture, and from human life under God, illustrate these truths.

Your conclusion will call people not only to believe great things about God, but to believe *in* this great and gracious Lord. "I believe in God through his Son Jesus Christ." I confide myself, and my dear ones, and my country, and my tomorrow, into his keeping, and join him in his invincible purpose. "I know whom I have believed, and am persuaded that he is able to keep that which I have committed unto him [and that means the future too] against that day" (II Tim. 1:12). He is able. He rules. He cares. He works quietly, ceaselessly, victoriously. Fret not about tomorrow. God holds tomorrow.

How to Run the Course

This topic may appeal as you and your people begin in earnest another year of work. Hebrews 12:1-3, as paraphrased by J. B. Phillips, is picturesque and provocative: "Surrounded then as we are by these serried ranks of witnesses, let us strip off everything that hinders, as well as the sin which dogs our feet, and let us run the race that we have to run with patience, our eyes fixed on Jesus the Source and the Goal of our faith. For He Himself endured a cross and thought nothing of its shame because of the joy He had in doing His Father's Will; and He is now seated at the right hand of God's Throne. Think constantly of Him enduring all that sinful men could say against Him, and you will not lose your purpose or your courage."

(1) How we run and where depends on that on which we fix our sights. "Let us run . . . looking to Jesus." (2) Let's get rid of the "impedimenta," the excess baggage, the stuff that trips us up. (3) Think constantly of his enduring the worst for us, and

triumphing over all, that we might have life beyond our wildest dreams. This will clarify your purpose and renew your courage.

Another approach to such a theme would be to answer the question, What difference would it make if I did keep Christ steadily before me? (1) Your aim will be clarified and your various purposes unified. (2) Your choices will be simplified. (3) You will find him providing the power to run the course to the end. He is " able to keep you from falling," from fainting, from giving up.

Jesus said, "all power is given unto me—
May know there is a God in Israel
I Sam 17-46
lest a worse thing come to thee
shew him how great things — Paul

TO LIVE?

the will to live
be going against
" Now one man
had lasted thirty-
had been ill for
your health re-
red indirectly by
treatment. Jesus'
ft your mat, and
s mat, and started

al living. Millions
ist they seem con-
e Charles Wesley's
: 10)? If you want
ent way to life that
is life indeed. What orders are issued as the divine Physician speaks to the chronic invalid? One of British Methodism's gifted leaders, Dr. Maldwyn Edwards, has suggested three directives which you could make the three emphases of a sermon on this theme:

I. *We must know where life is to be found.* As every " whodunit " author knows, and perhaps every criminal, most of us look for clues and missing treasure in hidden places. We miss what stares us in the face. Life is not to be found in strange, esoteric places or practices. You cannot earn it. It is God's gift. All men can have it by receiving it through trust and loving obedience. Where do you find this life eternal? As you confront God in Christ. "I came," he said, "that they may have life."

II. *We must enjoy it.* "What," asked John Wesley, "is the witness of the Spirit commonly called assurance?" Answer, "It is rest after labor, joy after pain, light after darkness." If we are no longer servants but sons, no longer slaves but friends and heirs,

> "Then let us rejoice
> In heart and in voice.
> Our leader pursue
> And shout as we travel the wilderness through."

You'd better not shout even for joy in our proper churches! Do we have just enough religion to make us miserable? Or do we commend our faith and our Lord by our infectious joy? A final tribute by the biographer of the late great Archbishop of Canterbury, William Temple, was the saying of a workingman who expressed his sense of loss by saying of the world church leader, "He was such a jolly man."

III. *We must explore the life God gives us* and wants us to live—to the full. This means that we must have firsthand acquaintance with what the church has called "the means of grace"—worship, the sacraments, the Christian community or fellowship, the continuous service with the cross at its heart. Would you really live? Then accept, enjoy, possess God's gift of life. "All [things] are yours, and you are Christ's, and Christ is God's" (I Cor. 3:22-23).

"The Best Is Yet to Be"

Have you preached to the middle-aged (anyone fifteen years older than yourself!) lately, or to persons moving into the ranks of those whom Paul Maves graciously calls "senior citizens"? Of course, unless you preach regularly in college or preparatory school chapels, you preach every Sunday to a congregation of which a large percentage is likely to be moving across the shadow line between young adults and older folk. Remember Ogden Nash's autobiographical lines:

"Middle-aged life is merry, and I love to lead it,
But there comes a day when your eyes are all right but your arm isn't long enough to hold the telephone book where you can read it,
And your friends get jocular, so you go to an oculist,
And of all your friends he is the joculist,
So over his facetiousness let us skim,
Only noting that he has been waiting for you ever since you said 'Good evening' to his grandfather clock under the impression that it was him."

Here is a Scriptural passage with preaching possibilities on this theme: "Then all the elders of Israel gathered together and came to Samuel at Ramah, and said to him, 'Behold, you are old and your sons do not walk in your ways; now appoint for us a king to govern us like all the nations.' But the thing displeased Samuel when they said, 'Give us a king to govern us.' And Samuel prayed to the Lord" (I Sam. 8:4-6).

That was telling the old man! Forgotten now was Samuel's long service. A new day demanded new leadership. Samuel suffered only from that recurring infirmity known in our time as "Anno Domini." Samuel's problem at that crisis in his career is more common than we suppose: it is the problem of handling advancing years. All ages should be concerned. The art of growing old successfully—Christianly—is one we ought to begin practicing by adolescence at the latest. Growing older may be an experience filled with tragedy and bitterness. For the Christian it ought to be one of hearty and deepening significance.

Once the struggle with himself was done, Samuel accepted his birthdays and gave himself to the new regime with whole-souled loyalty. The new leaders will not only have fair play from the retired veteran; they will have all Samuel's influence with God and with man.

I. *Accept the fact.* Here, then, is a rule for mastering the art of growing older: accept the fact of increasing birthdays without flinching, fear, or self-pity. Dr. J. A. Hadfield, British psychologist, has said: "A woman of fifty stays young if, when her children have grown up and left home, she advances to the next stage in her development and lets her interests broaden out and include the community. The business and professional men of sixty need never be 'on the shelf' if they leave the more active part of life to younger men, and seek to make their contribution to the community through their maturer wisdom and experience."

II. *Keep on the line of discovery.* As Samuel threw himself into the new kingdom and watched other, younger men occupy places of leadership once his, he kept that quality characteristic of youth: eagerness for new knowledge and new experiences. To keep youthful of spirit keep on the line of discovery. Samuel the aged founded a new theological seminary!

III. *Advancing years can mean increasing usefulness.* Think of the creative youngsters in their eighties and nineties today: Sir Winston Churchill, Grandma Moses, Bernard Baruch, *et al.* Immanuel Kant was seventy-four when he produced his *Metaphysics of Ethics.* John Wesley, when past eighty, was still preaching up and down England, saying with a smile, "'Tis time to live if I grow old."

IV. *Have a growing experience of God.* Most indispensable wisdom of all for making the later years the harvest years is to have a growing experience of God. "Samuel prayed to the Lord." Is there anything much more Christlike in the Old Testament than Samuel's response to the sentence imposed on him? "As for me, far be it from me that I should sin against the Lord by ceasing to pray for you; and I will instruct you in the good and the right way" (I Sam. 12:23). No wonder when Samuel had moved on into the unseen, his distraught successor frantically prayed the spiritualistic medium of Endor: " Bring up Samuel for me "!

To every soul who would live graciously the ageless Christ speaks.

> " Grow old along with me!
>   The best is yet to be,
> The last of life, for which the first was made:
>   Our times are in His hand
>   Who saith, ' A whole I planned,
> Youth shows but half; trust God: see all, nor be afraid.' "
>
> —*Robert Browning*

UNIVERSAL WEEK OF PRAYER

Prayer

What shall we preach about on the Sundays preceding Lent? Why not try sermons on one or all of the three subjects that led the survey conducted some time ago by the magazine *Guideposts*? Did you note the sermons that men and women across the country said they wanted most to hear? Three subjects received more than 60 per cent of the total vote. First in demand were sermons on "How can I make prayer more effective?" Second were pulpit messages to answer the question, "How can I make the greatest contribution to life?" Third (18 per cent) indicated a desire for preaching that would indicate "ways to increase religious faith." These preferences in the order named were submitted by "regular churchgoers." "Nonregular churchgoers" placed the last—on "ways to increase religious faith"—first, and sermons on prayer third. After these three subjects the following were in fourth and fifth places: "How religion can eliminate worrying" and "Happier families through religion."

You and I may be tempted to discount popular opinion polls. We may assert that the faithful preacher of the word must give people what they need and not what they want. Nevertheless, results of this survey are encouragingly close to the center of human need and to the Christian answer to it. Certainly sermons on these themes cannot be abstract, nor avoid facing what was once called the preacher's forgotten word, "How?" Here are some thoughts inspired by the subject.

How Can I Make Prayer More Effective?

Such a sermon should be addressed, not to those who are, as the Scots say, " far ben " — deeply within — the school of prayer, but to those who are beginners. " Five-finger exercises " in learning to play, and their equivalent in learning to pray, are elementary and indispensable. On such a theme, keep that man or woman steadily in view who may not need to hear convincing arguments on behalf of prayer's validity; most of our people readily acknowledge that prayer helps — or would help, if they knew how.

Into my office comes a student whose father's life has been profoundly shaken by the unexpected death of his wife. The father had always given at least vague assent to the main propositions of the Christian faith. He has been a nominal member of one of our churches. Now he desires earnestly to have firsthand acquaintance with God. With true discernment he senses that if he could pray meaningfully this would be experienced. His son asks, " What can I give him to read that would not be either too coldly theological or yet superficial and just pious? " More persons than we suspect are asking, as did the first company of the Lord's men: " Lord, teach us to pray " (Luke 11:1). The late Joseph Fort Newton's little book of prayers, *Altar Stairs,* contained this preface: " To all who, weary of seeking without finding, are willing to walk the quiet way of prayer." To such souls we would speak.

Do not overlook this other obvious fact: we speak most helpfully on prayer when we keep our Lord and his teaching and practice of prayer before us. However valuable much current " critical orthodoxy " may be (and I for one am grateful for its corrective, and for its recall to the dynamic center of the gospel), it must never cause us to minimize the Master as Teacher and Exemplar. Profitable for the preacher and for his preaching is a study of Christ's use of prayer, however fragmentary the Gospel record may seem to be.

This leads to a text for this particular sermon. Matthew 6:5-6 provides a specific answer, or part of the answer to the question,

" How? " J. B. Phillips' translation comes with freshness, even though the KJV and RSV remain best for the Scripture reading in the service. " When you pray don't rattle off long prayers like the pagans who think they will be heard because they use a lot of words. Don't be like them. After all God, who is your Father, knows your needs before you ask Him. Pray like this — "

Textually this passage is almost like the electronic-eye-operated doors — it opens itself.

I. *Be sincere in your praying.* Recall Jesus' picture of the man besieging as well as beseeching his neighbor for food when an unexpected friend comes to him at an inconvenient hour.

II. *Find a place where you may pray privately:* your own bedroom, a corner of some other room through which there is a minimum of household traffic, or a church, where environment and associations induce quietness and stimulate devotion.

III. *At first pray " privately,"* not only in the sense that your only audience is God, but in the way in which a child " tells it all " to a parent he has come to love and trust.

IV. *Pray definitely,* which generally means that our petitions should be brief, direct, simple. To " rattle off long prayers " inhibits clear thinking concerning our need and God's answer and will. Prayer is a two-way intercommunication system. If we only " send " lengthy messages, how can we " receive " the " signals," the messages from our divine Chief?

V. *Pray in the manner of the model prayer.* Of course, here you may well reserve fuller treatment for a series on the Lord's Prayer, but a few useful inferences from the prayer may help.

1. Recall and reaffirm the God in whom you believe. He is " our Heavenly Father," disclosed and brought near in Christ. An ancient principle reminds us that the rule of praying is the rule of believing. How we think of God determines our view of prayer. Thus do we honor or hallow his name, and deliberately create — as one of our theologians has written — " a spiritual milieu in

which an encounter with the living God may happen."

2. As honestly as you can, pray that God's rule may prevail, his will be done on earth as it is in heaven — beginning with you. Thereby we clear the channel for God's power to flow through us, even though its destination is likely to be other than we would choose.

3. Now you are ready to ask for what seems most necessary to your growth and peace. It may be, as Christ said, as mundane a petition as "Give us today the bread we need."

> "Thou art coming to a King
> Large petitions with thee bring."

As someone observed long ago, it is legitimate to pray for anything that it is legitimate to ask our Heavenly Father for.

4. Always ask for forgiveness and for "forgivingness." At our best we are sinners, penitent and forgiven sinners by his abundant grace.

Is the foregoing too much for one sermon of twenty or twenty-five minutes? We could preach two or three sermons on these aspects and not exhaust their significance.

Effective Prayer

Another type of sermon to answer this question might have three main divisions:

I. *Preparation*. This would include moral and psychological preparation. Of course, in one sense we cannot adequately prepare, nor do we need to prepare. He is already "beforetime with my soul." We should not seek him had we not in a measure found him, and been found by him. Yet recall Jesus' story of the man invited to a wedding and the reception after, who did not bother to prepare himself (Matt. 22: 11-14). We do need to "fling off the dirty clothes of the old way of living" (see Eph. 4: 22-23). Christ gave a clear directive here when he said we must leave our gift at the altar and attend to any unfinished business with our brother from whom we may be estranged (Matt. 5: 23-24). Next comes the mental or psychological preparation. We must deliberately divest ourselves of tensions, irrelevances, and preoccupations, if we would tune in to the central station. Will television sets suggest an illustration of this?

II. *Imagination.* "I keep the Lord always before me," said the writer of Ps. 16:8. Did he not do it as we must by an act of imaginative faith? Pictures and symbols help many to do this. Others find they can turn in a moment within an invisible chapel or quiet room built by imagination "inside." Retreating within, they picture themselves waiting for the divine Guest who is also Host. At first, and often thereafter, distractions come; uninvited "guests" knock at our chapel doors. These are told to wait until he comes whose presence brings light to find solutions, healing to restore our hurt souls, power to follow him on the daily trek. Always to the seeking and waiting soul he comes. Sometimes it will be true as in another upper room long ago, "The doors being shut . . . , Jesus came and stood . . . and said . . . , 'Peace be with you'" (John 20:19).

III. *Participation.* We must be receptive to his coming and responsive to his leading. He will show us tasks we must do with him and for him. This will include faithful participation in his community's worship week by week, in Kingdom projects, in tasks he has undertaken to accomplish on our planet. "You are my friends," he said, "if you do what I command you." That which he commands he makes known in the Scriptures, through his spirit operating through his body, the church, through the same spirit enlightening and directing our consciences. So does prayer become effective.

Getting the Habit of Prayer

"Evening, and morning, and at noon, will I pray" (Ps. 55:17). Let the words provide the structure or plan: (1) at our earliest waking moment, (2) at the center of the busiest day, and (3) at day's end, since only God can finish any day for us rightly — with evil canceled and covered, good accepted and confirmed, his peace bestowed, and active when we are not.

Christ's Portrait of God

Here is a series suggested by the Bible Reading Fellowship. Using Matthew's version of what some prefer to call the Disciples' Prayer, the series might be called "Christ's Portrait of God." He whom the New Testament calls "the image of the invisible God" drew word pictures of the great God. For the series of seven sermons, Matt. 6:9-13 provides the Scripture.

I. *God as Father* (see also Luke 11:5-13). When the word "God" is said, what picture flashes across the screen of your mind? Jesus used the name "Father" at the beginning of his ministry (Luke 2:49), through the stormy days that led to Calvary (John 12:27), and at the end (Luke 23:46). To him God was holy, fatherly Love. Does such a concept make for an easy-going familiarity with the Most High God? Does it not combine authority with tenderness? If God is the Father of our Lord Jesus Christ, what difference should it make in our basic attitudes toward life, our fellow humans, our work, death, and the moral issues of our time? What does it imply for the family?

II. *God as King* (see also Luke 11:14-23). God as Father is one facet. God as Sovereign is the other facet or aspect of the one reality. The phrase, "Who art in heaven," provides the key to this aspect of the divine nature. Our neo-orthodox theologians remind us that God is "the wholly other." We cannot be "pally" with the Lord of the worlds, the Creator of the universe, and the Ruler of history. His divine nature is to be hallowed and revered. "This sense of the holiness and majesty of God is the antiseptic element in our religion which saves it from lapsing into an easy sentimentalism." Even those who are convinced republicans as far as governmental systems are concerned need to rethink this idea of the divine Kingship. God's reign was one of our Lord's chief themes. This reign is at hand because Christ came, even though its consummation may be beyond history. Why was he sure? Because men wrecked by disease and sin are made whole by Christ's agency among them. Therefore we must pray with urgency, "Thy kingdom come," and assume our share in helping God to make actual the reign of God here and now, always confident that, with God, what should be shall be, and that this world's realms shall become the "kingdom of our Lord and of his Christ."

III. *God as Governor* is the third aspect of God that the prayer illumines. Matthew 21:28-32 is collateral reading. The phrase here is, "Thy will be done." How are we to pray this? In pious resignation to the inevitable, or in glad assent to the doing of God's plan? Surely the latter is indicated. It is our "Amen!" to God's purpose for us and for his world. (See what Paul calls God's will in Rom. 12:2.) To accomplish this will may be hard and costly. It may lead the disciple, as it did his Master, to a Gethsemane and to a Calvary.

IV. *God as Provider* emerges out of the petition for life's basic things: food, forgiveness, guidance, deliverance from evil. Day-by-day trust in God's providence is what we are told to pray for; not for the distant future, but for the day and for tomorrow. For commentary, read carefully the suggested passage, Matt. 6:25-34. Here is Christ's antidote to anxiety. Jesus' explanation of worry is that it is due to practical atheism and a lack of trust in the Father. "I will trust" the Father of Jesus and my Father, "and not be afraid."

V. *God as Pardoner*. In preparing this message, Matt. 6:14-15 is clearly suggested. "Forgive us . . . as we also have forgiven." This is no bargain between men and God. It means that my unforgiving spirit blocks the channel through which God's forgiving love comes. Repentance is the road to forgiveness. Consider the parable of the unforgiving servant (Matt. 18:23 ff.). So important is this teaching that vs. 14 and 15 are added to the Lord's Prayer to reinforce its teaching. See also Matt. 5:23-24, in which Jesus urges reconciliation with one's estranged brother before engaging in divine worship. Is the use of the word translated

" debts " telling us that the Christian sins chiefly through omission — or lack of thought and of imagination — as well as through failure to appreciate the other person's needs and viewpoints?

VI. *God as Guide* (see also Luke 22: 39-46). " Lead us not into temptation." Some temptations test and strengthen character (James 1: 2-3). Then we " welcome each rebuff that turns earth's smoothness rough," as Robert Browning bade. But what of the other type of temptation? If your physical resistance has been weakened by illness or accident, you would be asking for trouble if you walked into a room filled with germs. Christ knew this. He prayed that in the crisis his men would not enter into temptation. This prayer recognizes our frailty. It also acknowledges our dependence on One who " will not suffer you to be tempted above that ye are able; but will with the temptation also make a way to escape, that ye may be able to bear it " (I Cor. 10: 13).

VII. *God as Deliverer* (read also Matt. 1: 18-21). " Deliver us from the evil one." From many evils we have been and are being delivered, but not, as far as one can see, by God. From fear of poverty through unemployment, or sickness, or old age, the modern welfare state delivers its citizens. But no social arrangement and no state, however enlightened, can deliver us from certain recurrent and deep evils. Not ignorance, as the Greeks thought, but sin — this stubborn, profound wrongness in us — is our archfoe. From this tyranny we must have more than human deliverance. (For a commentary on this petition, read the words of the realistic Paul in Eph. 6: 10-18.)

How to Get What We Want from God

Take delight in the Lord, and he will give you the desires of your heart. . . . Trust in him, and he will act.

PSALM 37: 4.

Of course, our wants must be our true desires. They must be " screened " by the mind and spirit of Christ. If we first make

God and the doing of his will our delight, then we shall desire the best and our gracious God will give it "exceeding abundantly above all that we ask" (Eph. 3:20). What do we really want? How does God supply it? How can we "make God's interests our interests"?

God's Refusals

"Let it suffice you; speak no more to me of this matter" (Deut. 3:26). God sometimes says no to our most earnest prayers. Think of Moses on the threshold of the Promised Land; of Saint Paul's thrice-repeated beseeching for deliverance from his "stake in the flesh." Think of the prayers you offered to which God seemed to say "No," or, "Not yet." Can we not help our people to accept the unacceptable as from Love's hand? Can we not believe and help others to believe that when divine denial seems to be our experience, he generally shows us something else to do, something else to receive?

A poet named Mary Russell Olivant was quoted in *The Methodist Recorder* as saying:

> "And if, great Father, when I pray,
> Thy answer can be only, Nay,
> Still thou wilt comfort me and bless,
> With visions of thy righteousness."

The Meaning of Unanswered Prayer

One of my spiritually gifted Scottish friends, Dr. George Johnstone Jeffrey, once suggested a sermon on "The Meaning of Unanswered Prayer," and used the unusual text of Heb. 11:40: "God having provided some better thing for us." Consider these points for such a theme: (1) Life is discipline in learning to walk by faith; therefore, trust God. (2) Through our own frustrations God may be working out some wonderful purpose for others. (3) The grace of God can turn a material disappointment into a spiritual triumph.

III

EPIPHANY

Season of the Evangel

EPIPHANY

The Christian and the World

Epiphany, with its festival of lights, gives Albert Pennybacker a suggestion from the words in Phil. 2:15-16: "In which you appear like stars in a dark world, offering men the message of life" (Goodspeed). His two main points are: (1) Christians are not of this world, but they are in this world. (2) The Christian relationship to this world is that of stars: (*a*) The dark world needs light. (*b*) Stars give light. (*c*) Stars give guidance.

"Light My Candle"

Since the word "Epiphany" derives from a Greek word meaning "manifestation" or "showing forth," it is an ideal time for candlelight services. Such services should have at least a brief meditation on some aspect of the Light of the World. Suggested themes and texts follow.

"For thou wilt light my candle: the Lord my God will enlighten my darkness" (Ps. 18:28). (1) This is man's plea down the ages. The Bible is a record both of man's yearning for illumination and of the assurance and direction divine enlightenment brings. Scripture begins with "And God said, Let there be light." The epilogue describes the Holy City alight with God's glory — "For the Lord God giveth them light." (2) Epiphany, originating in the Eastern church in the third century, reminds us of God's response to man's cry for light. Born amid the shadows of a pagan world was One who has been a "light to lighten the Gentiles, and the glory of thy people Israel." (3) This prayer still ascends in this year of danger and opportunity. The lamp of hope, of peace, of understanding among races and between East and West must be lighted. God gives us the "Light of the World, undimming and unsetting, Who shines each mist away." (*a*) Christ is the Light upon the heart of God; (*b*) upon the nature and value of man; (*c*) upon life's dark problems; (*d*) upon the Unseen into which our loved ones vanish. As the Parsi interpreter said to the Bahaist who said that Jesus, Buddha, and Confucius were alike windows through which the Sun shone: "I beg to differ from the lady. Jesus is not just a window. He himself is the Sun shining through all the windows." "I am the light of the world."

"When the Light Goes On"

". . . that you may declare the wonderful deeds of him who called you out of darkness into his marvelous light." Unceasing war between goodness and evil causes blackouts. When will the light go on? Peter broadcasts a communiqué from headquarters: "The Light is on! You belong to it, to him! You have been called from the darkness of paganism into his marvelous light." Armed with this confidence we go out into the unknown to realize splendid possibilities. What kind? Look at four luminous lives and the hope each provides for us: (1) Peter in the marvelous light of the transfiguration (Matt. 17:1-9). (2) Paul on the road to Damascus (Acts 9:1-8). (3) John on his prison-island (Rev., ch. 1). (4) Stephen at the hour of his intense trial and victorious death (Acts 6:8 to 7:60).

A Series After Epiphany

Three sermons after Epiphany could use the familiar phrases: "He came" (Mark 2:17); "He saw" (John 6:5); "He conquered" (Rev. 6:2).

YOUTH WEEK

Today's Youth and Tomorrow's World

For a relevant and picturesque Biblical passage, see Moffatt's translation of I Sam. 14:1, 6, 23: "One day Jonathan the son of Saul said to his young armour-bearer, 'Come on, let us cross over the Philistine garrison on the other side.' But he did not tell his father. . . . 'The Eternal [said Jonathan] never has any difficulty about delivering his people, by means of many or by means of few.' . . . So the Eternal delivered Israel that day."

Here was a young man who wanted action and got it. He loved his country and longed to deliver it from the power of its enemies. This prince of the blood conceived a daring plan. With a young companion he carried it out. Both knew that the divine factor must operate to bring it off. God and audacious youth won the victory.

Can youth do it again? Do youth seek action or specious security? Today's youth, like Jonathan long ago, have inherited a warring world—against foes within and without the nation. One whom Isaac Watts called "the young Prince of Glory" calls to an engagement very dangerous and immensely thrilling. Do youth take their elders into their confidence? When they do, do we older people quench their ardor and trample their dream, or hearten them onward? "But he did not tell his father." Tomorrow's world could be more Christian, and, therefore, more just and more peaceable, if youth joined age and both joined Christ in an audacious enterprise.

When David Livingstone addressed the young undergraduates of Cambridge University on December 4, 1857, his scars spoke eloquently. So did his words: "Gentlemen, I beg to direct your attention to Africa. Do you carry out the work which I have begun. I leave it with you." To youth today the Lord Christ speaks, pointing not only to Africa but to America and to the world, beginning where we live: "I leave it with you." But he always adds a word no other pioneer can: "I am with you all the days and all the way."

Youth the Deliverer

(Scripture: I Kings 20:13-14)

Here is one passage that the Revised Standard Version may have "ruined" for the preacher whose imagination has been kindled by the King James Version's use of the phrase "the young men of the princes of the provinces." In the RSV this is replaced by "the servants of the governors of the districts." Without engaging in debate with Old Testament scholars, it seems reasonable still to suppose that servants of the governors would be young. When Ahab was assured that God would deliver a "great multitude" of enemies into his hands, he asked, "By whom?" And the prophet answered, "Thus says the Lord, By the young men under the commanders of the provinces." When the king looked over his forces, he failed to count the youth. A handful of young men made the difference in that ancient war.

A handful of Christian young people can make the difference between victory and defeat in today's spiritual warfare. Youth delivered our nation and many nations from bullies and their cohorts in World War II. Youth in Christ's service can deliver the community from the enemies of its peace and health and true life now.

How will youth deliver the world from the Ben-hadads who walk up and down seeking whom they can devour today? By accepting a few clear directives contained in the manual we call the Bible.

I. *Believe in yourself* at your present age. Here's the New Testament directive: "Let no one despise your youth, but set the believers an example in speech and conduct, in love, in faith, in purity" (I Tim. 4: 12). Youth may lack the wisdom of long experience. But youth has something that age rarely possesses: daring, vision, courage. An eighteen-year-old lad named Perkins revolutionized the dye industry by discovering aniline dye. Louis Pasteur at twenty was on the road to the century's greatest discovery. Einstein began his work at eighteen. Liverpool Cathedral, "the world's most perfect Gothic cathedral," was planned by Gilbert Scott, who won the prize with his plan when he was twenty-one. And history's supreme crusade was launched by "the young Prince of Glory," probably before he reached thirty years of age. The apostles when they first enlisted in Christ's service were not venerable, but valorous young messengers.

II. *Learn to "take it"* for Christ's sake and the Kingdom. Not just badges, honors, prizes. A famous leader of the early church said to his young assistant Timothy: "Take your share of suffering [hardness] as a good soldier of Christ Jesus" (II Tim. 2: 3). "We can take it," said the first young followers: "Lord, we are able." God has prepared us in advance to endure the worst and to use it for good purposes. We are never tested beyond our power.

III. "*Follow the Leader*." The third rule for delivering the besieged fortress of mankind from bullies and tyrants is this: "Follow the Leader." When you played the game of that name, you knew you could do what your leader did. So it is with the supreme Leader. Quote Heb. 12: 1-2: "Let us run, . . . looking to Jesus." He goes ahead and yet is always beside his followers. Always he stands by, present but unseen. And to follow him is to be delivered and to be a deliverer.

"White Captain of my soul, lead on;
I follow thee, come dark or dawn.
Only vouchsafe three things I crave:
Where terror stalks, help me be brave!
Where righteous ones can scarce endure
The siren call, help me be pure!
Where vows grow dim, and men dare do
What once they scorned, help me be true!"

— *Robert Freeman*

PRESENTATION OF JESUS IN THE TEMPLE

This Is Your Life — in Three Scenes

Lord, now lettest thou thy servant depart in peace, according to thy word; for mine eyes have seen thy salvation.

LUKE 2:29-30.

Part of "the beautiful afterglow of the birth of our Lord" relates to Jesus' presentation in the Temple forty days after his birth. Recall the others "in church" that day when Joseph and Mary brought the young child. Two elderly saints, Anna and Simeon, were in the congregation. Simeon, of whom the neighbors must have said, "A saint if ever there was one," perceived the tremendous significance of the child Jesus. Taking him in his arms, he cried the words familiar to millions across the centuries and known to many by the Latin "*nunc dimittis*." Joseph and Mary, astounded by this response of Simeon, were blessed and informed of the decisive effect of their boy upon "many in Israel" and upon his mother's soul.

Says David John Donnan: "This dramatic story is not only the record of a historical event in the life of our Savior; it is in epitome what I like to think of as 'The Drama of Life in Three Scenes.'" Here are the scenes:

Scene I. The things that are seen.
Scene II. The things that are unforeseen.
Scene III. The things that are unseen.

In the incarnation of Christ, the things that are seen were predominant in the Christmas story: the annunciation, the rest on the road to Bethlehem, Joseph's dream, the birth, the angels' song to the shepherds, the three Wise Men, and the flight into Egypt.

Next, and related to these events, was the drama of the unforeseen. How could Joseph and Mary foresee the tremendous events that were to overtake them? How could the shepherds have dreamed that they were to be the human audience of such heavenly sights and sounds? How could Herod have anticipated the threat carried by the arrival of the helpless infant?

Thirdly, "it is the unseen that dominates every scene." "We look," wrote Paul some years after the first Christmas, "not to the things that are seen, but to the things that are unseen; for the things that are seen are transient, but the things that are unseen are eternal." "By the unseen, of course, we mean the presence of the eternal God."

Now turn to the drama of everyman's life in the light of "the greatest drama in the world."

First, the things that are seen are important. How much do we see in (1) God's created world, (2) the world of persons, and (3) opportunities for Christian service?

Next, think of the ministry of the unpredictable in life lived "under God." Chance, luck, and the unforeseeable operate to bring adverse situations, but the unpredictable may produce spiritual and moral surprises of worth. Consider the mysterious workings of God's providence in a person's life.

Thirdly, life's drama reaches its climax when we realize that a constant, transforming, and guiding power is working in this guided and guarded universe. For the Christian, the Lord's promise is marvelously fulfilled. Christ is with him always. True, "we walk by faith, not by sight," but we do get help to find the right road and the power to travel it.

BROTHERHOOD WEEK

How Is All Your Care?

But a Samaritan, as he journeyed, came to where he was; and when he saw him, he had compassion . . . and took care of him. LUKE 10: 33-34.

When he saw the crowds, he had compassion for them, because they were harassed and helpless, like sheep without a shepherd. MATTHEW 9: 36.

While visiting the Canadian capital of Ottawa, I was greeted by an old friend whose first question was in the almost quaint idiom of an earlier day: " How is all your care? " He was solicitous for the well-being of members of my family. It is a good question for Christians. How is all our care? How many does it include? For what do we really care? Contrast the current comment, " I couldn't care less." Centuries ago, a Roman official lived in the presence of great issues with similar indifference and cynicism. " And Gallio cared for none of those things " (Acts 18: 17).

I. *What we care for shows whether we are growing Christians,* or suffering from arrested development. An elderly citizen who said, " I get up, read the obituary columns, and if my name isn't there, I go back to bed," was already spiritually extinct, or nearly so!

II. *What a community cares most about is an index of its genuine Christianity*. The test of any society is what it permits to happen to individuals. A test of a "great church," whatever its numerical strength, lies here: What happens to individuals within the fellowship? How wide are the bounds of our caring? The minutes of the Milford, Connecticut, town meeting, held in the year 1640, record an interesting action: "Voted, first, that the earth is the Lord's and the fullness thereof. Voted, second, that the earth is given to the saints. Voted, third, that we are the saints."

III. *When a man, a woman, or a group are "in Christ," they couldn't care more for individuals everywhere.* And as a result they live from a great depth of being within an ever greatening world. "We know that we have passed from death unto life, because we love the brethren" (I John 3: 14).

THE TRANSFIGURATION

Down to Earth

And the angel said to him, "Dress yourself and put on your sandals."

ACTS 12:8.

Life has a disconcerting habit of throwing us from the heights to the plains. God leads us to the summit only to lead us again into the valley, where need waits. Consider, for instance, Peter and the transfiguration experience. So it was, also, during Peter's escape from prison, as is vividly related in Acts, ch. 12. To have the chains miraculously struck from his wrists and then to hear the mundane command to get dressed and be sure to tie on his shoes is like being called from a marriage ceremony to answer the telephone.

I. *Linking the fact of God with the commonplace duties of life* is characteristic of the religion of revelation. Of course, Christ's primary gift is the breaking of "the power of canceled sin." He sets the prisoner free. He also gives grace to accomplish the transfer from vision to practice. He enables the disciple to "skirmish with each small unimportant thing." If we despise the frequently dull discipline of everyday jobs, we miss the meaning and glory of the gospel. "Fill the waterpots," "Go, wash in the pool of Siloam," said the Lord of life. "Take up thy bed, and walk." Could anything be more commonplace? "Dress yourself and lace your shoes," said the heavenly liberator to the apostle.

II. *Our Lord himself accepted this test* and subjected himself to this kind of discipline. Matthew reports the sequel to the Master's hilltop teaching hour: "When he was come down from the mountain," he confronted a leper. "I will," said Jesus; "be thou clean." From the high politics of God's Kingdom he moves to the parochial. From the heights he comes to the lower levels where men and women are hurt, and he experiences their deep sense of need. This is where we find him today. If he came not down from the mountain "to heal these hearts of pain," to transact God's business where the humblest citizen lives, would his gospel be good news for common folk?

If our Lord met this test and demonstrated this kind of religion, we too must accept his grace to come "down to earth." After the angel opens locked doors, there are shoes to be tied, old roads to be traveled, the duty lying nearest us to be tackled. Of course we grow tired of the old routine. "O for the wings of a dove, or even of a small plane!" we sigh or even pray. And then comes the deeper insight of a picturesque preacher of an earlier day. Said Father Stanton, "If God gave us all we asked for, I should think we should most of us be in hell by this time." Henry van Dyke's lines are apposite:

"Every task, however simple,
Sets the soul that does it free;
Every deed of love and kindness
Done to man is done to Thee."

III. *Peter found assurance that his experience was no dream* when he obeyed the simple directive. He found that, in his coming down to earth's humble assignments, the Master had come and called for him. "I come in little things, saith the Lord." In his parable of the pounds, Jesus put on the nobleman's lips a word which the King James Version translates, "Occupy till I come." Literally it may mean, "Get busy and keep busy until I return." It is like our Lord to say some such word.

Some years ago when the original company of *The Green Pastures* was playing in New York City, Wesley Hill, the actor who played Gabriel in that remarkable play, was killed by a taxicab. The event stirred the blasé city as few things could do. Richard B. Harrison, famous player and fine Christian layman who played the "Lawd," joined the other members of the cast at the funeral chapel. As they looked on the silent form of their friend, he said, "Now, Gabe, you look after things till we come." And the other actors, looking at Gabriel's unmoving lips, made his usual reply, "O.K., Lawd."

IV

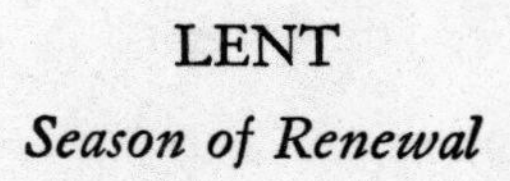

LENT

Season of Renewal

LENT

Certainly in the season of Lent and at Easter we announce the dawn of God's eternal day by which the shadows of sin and death are banished. Among the key words of the gospel are "light" and "life," with their companions "hope" and "salvation." "The dayspring from on high hath visited us" (Luke 1:78) we sang at Christ's Nativity. He has given a "light to lighten the Gentiles" (Luke 2:32). Throughout the weeks commemorating his last pilgrimage, the darkness deepens, but as we keep close to this Man of sorrows and of joy we know that he is indeed the Light of the World, and that the darkness has never put out that marvelous light. "If we walk in the light, as he is in the light, we have" (I John 1:7) more than we can ask or dream.

How to Keep Lent

The aim of the Christian discipline is the love that springs from a pure heart, from a good conscience, and from a sincere faith.

I TIMOTHY 1:5 (MOFFATT).

One fairly obvious and fruitful treatment of this theme is to follow the text's own divisions: (1) by cultivating love that springs from a heart made pure by God's forgiveness and the spirit's occupancy. (2) By a good conscience, that is one which, being cleansed of both unrighteousness and self-righteousness, is sensitive to human need, to injustice, to moral issues in our society. (3) By affirming a sincere faith. This is primarily what is meant by trust in the great God who has drawn near in his Son Jesus Christ, but it also includes a working creed through which a spiritual experience is expressed.

My suggestion, however, is to deal first, by way of introduction, with the approach or arrival of the Lenten season, and by defining it as simply and clearly as possible. It is the forty-day period when many Christians turn aside, more frequently than at other times, to follow devotionally the pilgrimage of Christ in " his high, pitiful journey " to the cross.

Those who are in so-called nonliturgical branches of Christ's church may suspect an emphasis upon good works. Formalism in religion, reliance upon ritual rather than upon righteousness, is a persistent error and menace to vital Christian living. Recall Amos' remarks upon similar instances of externalism in Amos 5:21–24.

Lent should mean — and does mean to many sincere disciples — much more than relief from a dizzy social whirl. It is more than a recess in which to attend to moral manicuring. In a world in which alternation is a principle not to be lightly disregarded, Lent may provide for the Christian a season for recovering of perspective, renewing of spiritual vitality, and regaining focus in worship.

Here a brief account of how the season began may be of interest. Eventually the fast was fixed at forty days to correspond to Christ's wilderness fast prior to his temptation. Shrove Tuesday, the day before Lent's actual beginning, takes its name from the fact that penitents were " shriven," or given absolution for their sins, on that day. Ash Wednesday, as most Protestants now know, is named from an old, pre-Christian custom of sprinkling ashes on the head to denote contrition. Christ left no instructions for keeping fasts. But he did participate in the religious ceremonies of his time. He journeyed to Jerusalem to keep festivals. He did lay down one condition concerning observances: " When you fast, be not as the hypocrites " (Matt. 6:16). We are not to be play actors in religion.

I. *Lent may be kept as a time of growth in Christian faith and character.* Is Christianity not a discipline as well as a doctrine? So in our text Paul reminds his young colleague Timothy. A world leader of the Christian movement declared, "The future of the world is in the hands of disciplined people." Even the church's enemies would accept that observation. "The love that springs," that is artesian, that overflows from the deep reservoir of God's love and truth, supplies the motive power.

How shall we keep Lent? Three rules for the road of our pilgrimage with Christ to the cross and its Easter sequel follow.

II. *Let us keep Lent constructively.* Honest dealing with ourselves often involves destructive operations. When in Britain I read of a call for a demolition squad. Men were needed to root out and destroy an old, unexploded Nazi bomb buried deep in a London area. Jesus said something about plucking out that which offends, resolutely rooting out that which hinders our growth in maturity. In *My Dear Ego,* a book for teen-agers and others, Dr. Fritz Kunkel makes clear that we cannot be the kind of persons God wants us to be until we face two questions: First, what is the goal of our striving? Secondly, what puts us into the "doghouse" of despair and gives us a sense of defeat? In Lent let us each one deal constructively with the one person who gives us the most trouble: our own self. Someone sagely observed: "There are seven deadly sins. The first is dishonesty; the other six are selfishness. But the seven are then one: self-centeredness."

III. *Let us keep Lent compassionately.* This is more than pity toward other members of the family who watch you suffer from your temporary abstinence from tobacco or candy! Compassion means suffering with another. Christ's compassion for the multitude issued from his identification with them in their plight. It moved him to help them. To enter into the fellowship of Christ's sufferings is more than an emotional experience. It means the moral equivalent of prayer and fasting: deep concern and an acceptance of responsibility to remake the conditions that create hell for others. Consider Isaiah's searching word: "Is not this the fast that I have chosen? to loose the bands of wickedness, to undo the heavy burdens, and to let the oppressed go free, and that ye break every yoke? Is it not to deal thy bread to the hungry, and that thou bring the poor that are cast out to thy house? when thou seest the naked, that thou cover him; and that thou hide not thyself from thine own flesh?" (Isa. 58:6-7). Immense returns from such costly investment of one's self are promised by the same prophet: "Then shall thy light break forth as the morning, and thine health shall spring forth speedily." True health is the consequence of "the love that springs from a pure heart, from a good conscience, from a sincere faith."

IV. *Let us keep Lent secretly and cheerfully.* "When you fast," said the Lord of life, "do not put on a gloomy look, like the hypocrites, for they neglect their personal appearance to let people see that they are fasting. I tell you, that is all the reward they will get. But when you fast, perfume your hair and wash your face, so that no one may see that you are fasting, except your Father who is unseen, and your Father who sees what is secret, will reward you" (Matt. 6:16-18). Have we not resented a person admiring the sunset who also wanted to be admired admiring the sunset? When you look at the spinning propeller of a piston-driven plane, you can look straight through the blades, so fast and so rhythmical is the motion. The aim of Christian discipline is so to hide itself that all that appears is spontaneous. When others look for it or at it, they look through it — through us — to the One to whom we are bound with ties of love and service. "Good" people repel others by their pious melancholy, their look of painful virtue. Christian living is serious, not solemn; merry, not flippant; winsome, not woebegone.

To keep Lent, keep company with Him who for the sake of others disciplined, consecrated, and sanctified himself. Someone may take knowledge of us that we have been with Jesus and say what the Earl of Kent said to King Lear in exile: "You have that in your countenance which I would fain call master."

Do We Still Need a Savior?

Do we need health? (Indicate the common roots of the two words "Savior" and "health.") Do we need deliverance from our enemies — sin, guilt, meaninglessness, death? Years ago the Harvard philosopher W. E. Hocking declared that there was more lostness in the world than ever before.

I. *What does the New Testament mean by "salvation"?* Use the three picture phrases employed by Paul to answer this question: redemption, justification, and reconciliation. Rescue them from being abstractions. Redemption pictures a captive being set free; justification shows a guilty man being acquitted; reconciliation shows an estranged and rebellious child being welcomed back and restored to his parents' confidence and love (Col. 1: 14; Gal. 3: 13; 4: 5; Rom. 3: 24; 6: 18; 8: 2).

II. *What does Christianity declare to be our jailer,* our condemnation, our estrangement? Consider the Biblical doctrine of sin — not just sins, plural.

III. *How are we saved?* By God in Christ taking our sin upon him. Love divine and eternal breaks the power of sin, ending the separation our sin has made, mediating forgiveness.

How Christ Saves Us

Therefore, since we are justified by faith, we have peace with God through our Lord Jesus Christ. Through him we have obtained access to this grace in which we stand, and we rejoice in our hope of sharing the glory of God.

ROMANS 5: 1-2.

One present-day New Testament scholar states that Paul's whole doctrine of salvation is contained in these two verses. In these words we have Christianity's most trustworthy exponent telling us that the salvation God has wrought is, as Dr. Lightfoot, the famous Biblical theologian, said, "a thing of the past, a thing of the present, and a thing of the future." Why not let these be the divisions of your sermon? Think again of Rom. 5:1-2. (1) Paul looks back to the time when the believer received God's forgiveness in Christ. (2) He muses on his present blessedness, "this grace in which we stand." (3) He looks forward to the time when, sin and death being ended, he will enjoy the vision glorious: "We rejoice in our hope of sharing the glory of God."

Under the first heading, take yourself and your people back to Christ and his cross. Something was done there that needed to be done, that man could not do for himself, that need never be done again. Dr. A. M. Hunter asks that we study three passages to penetrate more deeply into Paul's thought about Christ's atoning death (Rom. 3:24 ff.; II Cor. 5:21; Gal. 3:13). Always the cross is linked with the resurrection (I Cor. 15:17; Rom. 4:25). "We are saved by the living crucified."

In such a message the preacher must anticipate the question that is likely to rise in at least a few minds: How does an event back in history become a living reality for me here and now? Of course the answer is that it is appropriated by faith. Faith is man's trusting and obedient response to God's gracious dealing with us in Christ. The true New Testament meaning is in Rom. 1:5, "The obedience which faith is." Nygren's word, in his commentary on Romans, is worth using: "When a man hears the gospel and is conquered by it, that is faith." Here Hunter is helpful when he clarifies the meaning of faith in five ways: (1) It is trust in a person, not in a proposition. (2) It is opposed to "works," to every doctrine of redemption by human effort (Gal. 2:16; 3:2; Rom. 4:5). (3) It is an act and an attitude of life (Rom. 10:9; Gal. 2:20): Christ "loved me and gave himself for me" joined with "The life I now live in the flesh I live by faith in the Son of God, who loved me and gave himself for me." (4) Faith is the Christian's "wedding ring," as Luther called it. It is union with Christ; it is to be in Christ mystically and morally (Rom. 6:3 ff.; Gal. 2:20; II Cor. 13:5; Eph. 3:17).

(5) This faith issues in good works, " for in Christ Jesus nothing external is of any avail, but faith working through love " (Gal. 5:6).

When you come to deal with salvation as a present and progressive experience, you will do as interpreters of the gospel have done before you — give meaning and power to the concept expressed by the frequently used New Testament phrases " in Christ " and " in the Spirit." Such teaching should show men that " being saved " involves vital membership in the community of the Spirit. " Christ and his people form a corporate fellowship, so that to be 'in Christ' means to be a member of that religious fellowship which draws its very life from Christ " (G. S. Duncan). Thus the church is not an option, but a necessity, if we would experience God's forgiveness, healing, welcome home, and all the rights, privileges, and responsibilities of membership in the family.

" We were saved," " We are being saved," and there is the third, the future tense of salvation, " We shall be saved." Emil Brunner's epigram is thought-kindling: to be a Christian is to share in " something which has happened, which is happening, and which will happen." True, the Kingdom has come; it is now. Already the believer is " translated out of the kingdom of darkness into the Kingdom of God's beloved Son." Yet in another sense, the Kingdom is to come. Salvation is to be completed. What is the apostle's Christian hope? Here again your study may confirm what our New Testament guide asserts. The heart of Paul's hope can be put in three words: " being with Christ " (Rom. 6:8; I Thess. 4:17; Phil. 1:23). Being with Christ means being " in Christ," which includes being like him, " conformed to the image of his Son " (Rom. 8:29).

Proud of This News

I am proud of the good news, for it is the power of God which produces salvation for everyone who believes, to the Jew first, and to the Greek. The way to a right relation-

ship with God is revealed in it when man's faith responds to God's fidelity, just as it stands written, "It is the man who is in a right relationship with God as a result of his faith who will live."

ROMANS 1:16-17 (WILLIAM BARCLAY).

Like the classical concertos, this Christian symphony of faith opens with a crashing chord. The theme is stated. More than one Christian scholar finds in these two verses the heart of Paul's gospel. We take it for granted that Paul was proud of the gospel. Yet think of what the gospel had brought to him by way of opposition, ridicule, persecution, and imprisonment. But there was something in the good news that made him invulnerable and victorious over the worst that could hit him.

As we move imaginatively into the crucial events of Christ's life, death, and resurrection, it is well to keep before us the "three great foundation pillars of Paul's thought and belief." These are the conceptions of salvation, faith, and justification. Let these three watchwords provide the threefold outline of the message. I owe Prof. William Barclay much for the insights of this discussion.

I. *Salvation*. When Paul wrote, men were searching for salvation as for no other treasure. Life had "tumbled in" around thoughtful persons. They sought deliverance and peace. Christianity offered them what they sought and desperately needed. Salvation was offered: (1) from physical illness (Matt. 9:21); (2) from danger (Matt. 8:25; 14:30); (3) from life's infection and from a crooked, perverse generation (Acts 2:40); (4) from lostness (Matt. 18:11; Luke 19:10); (5) from sin (Matt. 1:21); (6) from the wrath (not the anger) of God (Rom. 5:9); and (7) from the temporal and fleeting (Rom. 13:11; I Cor. 5:5; II Tim. 4:18; I Peter 1:5).

II. *Faith*. This rich word, as used in the New Testament, means: (1) loyalty—fidelity to the divine captain of salvation; (2) belief—the conviction that certain things are true; (3) the

Christian religion — the faith (II Cor. 13:5); and (4) most characteristically, total acceptance and total trust. This is total commitment to the God who has revealed himself and given himself in Christ.

III. *Justification.* This Biblical word has a different meaning from the ordinary English one. "He justified himself," we say, and we mean: "He gave reasons for his action, or decision, or opinion. He tried to prove he was right." But in this word Paul means that God is treating an outlaw as if he had never been an outlaw at all. God treats the sinner as a child to be loved. In justifying us, God treats us as a perfectly wise and loving father treats his child. Therefore, we enter into a new relationship with God. This relationship is one of confidence, love, and friendship, instead of suspicion, hostility, and fear. A man is in this relationship not because of anything he has done that could be called virtuous or meritorious; he is in this relationship of love because he has thrown himself in trust on the incredible mercy and love of God. Jesus has made this possible. God who seemed to be an enemy is shown to be our supreme Friend, our Savior. Who would not be proud of such good news?

Sky Hooks Monday Through Friday

But even though we were dead in our sins God was so rich in mercy that He gave us the very life of Christ (for it is, remember, by grace and not by achievement that you are saved), and has lifted us right out of the old life to take our place with Him in Christ in the heavens.

EPHESIANS 2:4-6 (PHILLIPS).

I. *Sky hooks are in widespread demand.* A thoughtful article by the assistant to the president of Standard Oil of Ohio was recently featured in the *Harvard Review of Business.* In this essay, Mr. Ohmann reiterates a plea that sky hooks — an abiding faith around which personality and the common life can be integrated and given meaning — must be found, not for weekends only, but for Mondays through Fridays. Supporting his contention that this represents the intensified search of modern man, he cites the unparalleled interest in religion, at least in the Western world.

II. *Something better than spiritual values is offered in Christian faith and experience.* God offers sky hooks through his self-revelation and self-giving in Christ. So Ephesians startlingly declares that God gave us, and gives us, " the very life of Christ . . . and has lifted us right out of the old life to take our place with Him in Christ in the heavens." You may helpfully rescue this phrase from pious rhetoric by showing your hearers that such heavenly places may be known now and not in some post-mortem period.

III. *Name three sky hooks!* (1) A great faith in which to believe — not a process in history and not a romantic set of self-help propositions, but the Christian creed. (2) An eternal society to belong to. " In Christ " means at least all that we mean by the living church, his body. As Pauline teaching stresses, the church is the resurrection society, despite its sinning and frailty. (3) The supreme cause to work for. The cause is God's Kingdom here and now, hereafter and forever, intimately and inwardly personal and yet inevitable and redemptively social. It is primarily God's gift to us, but we must also work with him for its fulfillment, since it is the rule of righteous, fatherly love in every human relationship.

IV. *How may these sky hooks be brought into office, factory, shop, and school, Mondays through Fridays.* (1) By living the life " in Christ " by our intelligent, ministrant, Christian love to fellow workers. (2) By participation in such enterprises devoted to more abundant life of all involved in the Monday-through-Friday operations as may be indicated to the Christian. (3) By intercessory prayer daily for all engaged with us.

What's Life All About?

(Scripture: Luke 19: 11-27)

I. *Introduction*. Life situation. A local tragedy destroyed the life and home of a widowed mother of two young children. She had made an unsuccessful attempt to overcome handicaps of temperament and circumstance. A middle-aged drugstore clerk, commenting on the situation, remarked: "Makes you wonder what life's all about, doesn't it? It doesn't seem to make any sense." Cite various attempts at interpreting life's enigmas. Seventeenth-century poet John Gay gave his sardonic verdict:

> "Life is a jest, and all things show it;
> I thought so once, but now I know it."

II. *Proposition*. The key to unlock the maze is in the Christian reading of life and history. This may be found in an allegorical use of the parable of the pounds as Luke tells it.

III. *Development or body of sermon*.

1. The fact of the divine initiative. "A certain nobleman [God in Christ] went into a far country to receive a kingdom" (RSV, "kingly power"). God not only is, but he is the divine seeker. At the heart of existence is power and wisdom and love, purposeful and personal. History is truly his story.

2. The fact of divine grace. "Calling . . . his servants, he gave them ten pounds, and said to them, 'Trade with these till I come.'" What is there that we have not received? We have talent, years, capacity to love and be loved, faith, and, supreme over all, God's gift of himself in his Son—the "givenness" of life, and our responsibility in the light of it.

3. The fact of the divine sacrifice to overcome man's rebellion. "But his citizens hated him, . . . saying, 'We do not want this man to reign over us.'" Like the boy of whom Dr. Walter Russell Bowie tells, men and women may admire and love this "nobleman" of Galilee and eternity, but many "just can't stand Jesus."

The cross is the symbol of our resistance and rebellion. It is also the light on the heart and action of God.

4. The fact of divine judgment and human accountability. "When he returned, having received the kingly power, he commanded these servants, to whom he had given the money, to be called to him, that he might know what they had gained by trading." He still comes in judgment, and the church's faith is that he will come at life's end and at the end of history. "What did you make of it?" is his question. His condemnation is directed to the steward who "played it safe." To hoard a God-given gift, to refuse to take a risk on behalf of the Kingdom, and to abandon cravenly the adventure of love brings its own hell. Here the analogy breaks down. Unlike the nobleman in Jesus' story, the great God with whom we have to do judges us with mercy and uncalculating love. But love's question can be more searching than that of any cold impersonal judge: "What did you do with what I have done for you?"

"A certain nobleman went into a far country to receive a kingdom." To read the "contradictions of history" and the tangled events of one's own life in terms of that journey is to make sense of life and to find meaning and splendor in it.

Hearing Aids

"He that hath ears to hear, let him hear" must have been said by our Lord more often than the Gospels report. When the Old Testament prophets gave their preview of God's golden age, they included among the messianic gifts restoration of hearing. Then "the ears of the deaf shall be unstopped" (Isa. 35:5). When Jesus sought to convince the puzzled John the Baptist that the Christ had indeed come, he cited as conclusive proof the fact that "the deaf hear" (Matt. 11:5).

This healing of the deaf has poignant appeal today. It is estimated that between ten and twenty millions of North Americans suffer from impaired hearing. Many specialists think that 50 per cent of us hear imperfectly. But much more distressing are those with normal physical hearing who are spiritually and morally deaf. Mark describes one of the divine physician's open-air clinics in Mark 7:34-37. Here are one preacher's main points:

I. *God himself must sigh as he observes our unnecessary spiritual deafness.* Here is our Father's world, vocal with melody and meaning. Yet only to the listening ears of the saint or poet "all nature sings," and round him "rings the music of the spheres." So many go through this glorious world as if a color film were being shown without the sound track.

II. *The Lord Jesus Christ is the supreme otologist,* the specialist who furnishes hearing aids to those whose spirits are dulled for one reason or another. He makes us hear overtones "on the other side of silence." How? By attuning our souls to the Maker of all things harmonious and beautiful.

> "Lord, I was deaf: I could not hear
> The thrilling music of thy voice;
> And now I hear thee and rejoice,
> And all thine uttered words are dear."

Thomas Carlyle, uncommonly blue even for the dour Scot, once complained, "Oh, that God would speak to us as he spoke to men of olden time!" But, by the Holy Spirit, God does speak—through Scripture, enlightened conscience, history's events, nature, and the living Lord. Insulation against noise is a boon to city dwellers, but insulation against hearing the "still sad music of humanity" is disastrous.

III. *We must train ourselves* through creative silence and through disciplined attentiveness to God's voice. Only then can we have deep understanding and joy in this mysterious and marvelous world. Joan of Lorraine, in Maxwell Anderson's play, said, "Up to the end my voices will speak to me." "Be still, and know that I am God," says the One who speaks in the voice of gentle stillness. Christopher Morley's "Private Enterprise" will prove useful in this sermon. Consider the closing words:

"In unimpassioned silence we might find
(If ever) What the Author Had in Mind."

Recall John's account of what the multitude heard when God spoke. Some said that "it had thundered"; others said, "An angel has spoken." Jesus said, "Father."

"Where one heard thunder, and one saw flame,
I only know He named my name."

What do you hear? The death rattle of our civilization and our culture, or the birth pangs of a new day? The roar of a purposeless machine, or the murmur of God's Kingdom coming without clamor or violence? Are you listening?

How's Your E.Q.?

Everyone has heard of the I.Q. But what of our energy quotient? Is our amount of drive dependent entirely on our constitution? Perhaps we have given up living on our constitution and are existing on the bylaws! Africans have a farewell greeting at evening: "Don't be tired tomorrow." But we are likely to be weary. We may not blame a vitamin deficiency, but a faith deficiency. For increase of vitality try the prophet's prescription in Isa. 40:29: "He gives power to the faint, and to him who has no might he increases strength." Waiting on God in prayer, in worship, in meditation, results in an increase in energy. God gives us:

I. *An upsurge of power*. We may not fly through the air with the greatest of ease, but we find wings given us for sunward climbing. Henry M. Stanley, explorer and discoverer of Livingstone, testified that prayer "lifted me hopefully over the one thousand five hundred miles of forest tracks, eager to face the day's perils and fatigues."

II. *Energy for running upon God's purposes is supplied*. Spurts are necessary. Difficult, intense toil is required. Men and women find that practicing God's presence keeps the batteries charged even when severe demands are made. But since most of us neither fly nor run, we need, and we find given us, energy as we link our lives with God.

III. *Power to walk the daily road.* To trudge undiscouraged and unweakened day after day, year after year, is one of the proofs of renewed life. The secret? "Our sufficiency is from God, who has qualified us to be ministers [servants] of a new covenant . . . in the Spirit; for . . . the Spirit gives life" (II Cor. 3:5).

If the Worst Comes to the Worst

What shall we then say to these things? If God be for us, who can be against us?

ROMANS 8:31.

What things? The kind of things to which Paul referred in vs. 18 through 25 of this same lyrical chapter. "The sufferings of this present time . . . this slavery to decay . . . groans and agonies. . . ." Yes, and the catalogue of troubles that follows the text: "tribulation, distress, persecution, famine, nakedness, peril, sword . . . death, life, angels, principalities."

I. *Here is Christian realism.* Let's face it, says the apostle. Life is like this. Paul looks at the worst, but he doesn't sit down and indulge in the cheap luxury of self-pity, nor does he wallow in the slough of despair. Have we this kind of dogged courage to face the grim, the "rugged," aspects and elements of life? Or do we dodge them, practicing evasive action on every front? Chesterton once said that the finest lines in English poetry are, "Over the hills and far away." Come May and June and we know what he means. How we'd like to "get away from it all" — go hiking on strange roads where around the next corner something thrilling may be waiting! But often around the corner there's a hill winding steeply, and at the hill's summit a cross. So that's life, moan the discouraged — a crucifixion. But surely, says the spiritual giant who is our guide into the truth of Christ, surely you have known that the cross is empty, that "from the ground there blossoms red life that shall endless be."

II. *Let's face the worst that could possibly happen,* and yet remember that with the worst there is the best, beside us and ahead of us. For always there is God, of whose love and forgiveness, of whose care and direction, we have had rich experience. Here the preacher could list the worst things that can overtake the Christian pilgrim: adversity, sickness, moral failure, bereavement, death. In every such possible experience and disaster there is always the infinite factor. And this infinite factor is not another "x"—an unknown quality or force. God has made himself known supremely in the life and personality, the teachings, death and resurrection of Jesus Christ. He has given us the community of the spirit in which we are surrounded by allies and friends, headed by the divine and invincible Leader.

A superb illustration is to be found in the experience of a great Scottish preacher, the late Dr. Arthur John Gossip, of Glasgow. When his wife was suddenly taken from him, he sounded for his people and for Christians everywhere the trumpet call of assurance. "When life tumbles in, what then?" Why, then, God as always, and where God is there cannot be despair or fear. More than twenty years ago the brilliant Prof. John Macmurray wrote in a book, *Freedom in the Modern World:*

"To the man who is afraid of poverty, religion does not say, 'God will save you from losing your money.' It says, 'Suppose you do lose your money, what is there to be afraid of in that?' If it is the fear of death and suffering that haunts you, real religion says: 'Yes, of course, you will die, but there is nothing to be afraid of in that.' It does not say, as all false religion says: 'Shut your eyes to things you are afraid of; pretend they don't exist, that there are ways and means of getting the divine powers on your side so that you will be protected from the things you are afraid of. They may happen to other people, but they will not happen to you. God will see to it that they don't.' On the contrary, real religion says: 'Look the facts that you are afraid of straight in the face; see them in all their brutality and ugliness; and you will find, not that they are unreal, but that they are not to be feared.'"

III. *Because God is with us*—not to give us immunity from "the slings and arrows of outrageous fortune," but to enable us to handle them—we develop skill in turning the worst into something better. This skill is produced by combined operations, by uniting faith and prayer with practical work and organization. In Neh. 4:9 is a master clue: "We made our prayer unto our God, *and* set a watch against them day and night."

When Dwight L. Moody and the then young John R. Mott planned their summer school at East Northfield, Massachusetts, it was said that they planned for the sessions as though there were no such thing as prayer, and they prayed as though there were no such thing as organizations. A modern missionary, Dr. D. C. Somervell, wrote of David Livingstone: "In every conceivable emergency, Livingstone could be relied upon to do two things: to say his prayers *and* take his astronomical bearings."

Martha and Mary, the practical type and the "spiritual" type, should live in the same person, and can. God expects us to handle many difficult assignments by ourselves, but he never leaves us alone to do them. Who said, "Lo, I am with you always, to the close of the age"? Has he ever broken his promise?

The following was written between the years 1515 and 1582 by Saint Theresa of Avila: "To give our Lord the perfect service, Mary and Martha must combine. The Lord, when you are busy in the kitchen, is beside you; he walks among the pots and pans." Robert Louis Stevenson wrote: "Quiet minds cannot be perplexed or frightened, but go on in fortune or misfortune at their own private pace like the ticking of a clock during a thunderstorm."

Violent Faith

From the days of John the Baptist until now the kingdom of heaven has suffered violence [or, *has been coming violently*], *and men of violence take it by force.*

MATTHEW 11:12.

In a time when many are enamored of a soporific form of Christianity, it is good to be reminded that in Christ's view violence and struggle have their place. Strive to enter in at the narrow gate. Be ready to mutilate your life if necessary. Rouse the whole household to get food for your friend. These violent directives came from our Lord.

In December, 1941, a brilliant lay preacher, Bernard Lord Manning, died. Afterward a sermon on this text was found among his writings. Here are his main points (slightly altered):

I. *Religion without struggle.* Many dislike religion because there seems no place in it for "healthy violence, hearty struggling, straining after greater powers." Common expositions of Christian faith exalt the virtues we like when we are not feeling well, such as resignation and meekness. This is wrong.

II. *Religion without peace.* So is the opposite interpretation, that religion is unwelcome because it is not soothing enough. Both are wrong, because both ignore this text. Christ gives peace, joy, and strength. He also promised hardness, self-denial, and a cross. Hardness is part of discipleship.

III. *What does this violent struggle mean for us?* Most of us are not of the heroic mold of the great saints. But there are two ways where we must expect to find it hard. Some take one way, some the other. (1) Some find faith hard. They wish the evidence for its truth were stronger. "Faith is not knowledge; it is easy to walk by sight and requires no trust." Recall the apostle Thomas. He was not sure of his Lord's triumph, but he gave him absolute loyalty. Faith is a fight for some honest souls. (2) Our own actions may be hard. Right action is hard for some disciples. But this kind of violence against temptation makes strong Christians. If we were never tempted, we could do little if anything for our Lord.

IV. *In faith, as in action, most of us need Christ's courage.* We want things too easy. The Christian is the man who "wants a situation that gives scope to the powers he has in Christ and from Christ." He has overcome. He calls us to share his triumph.

To do that we must use every barrier, every obstacle, as a chance to take the Kingdom of Heaven by force.

Wrestling Jacob

In seeking to match a word of God to the need of many persons, don't overlook this marvelous Old Testament story in Gen., ch. 32. Harris E. Kirk once published a long series of sermons on "The Jacob Saga." Dr. Kirk knew that Jacob's story is intensely modern. This character out of the misty past "speaks our language, meets our problems, looks out upon our world, and reacts toward life very much as we do ourselves." Even the stresses and strains of life today seem to be anticipated in this ancient narrative.

Deal faithfully with Jacob. He is not an admirable person. Deceiver and shrewd conspirator, he was at times a contemptible trickster. But this candid snapshot of his strange wrestling match at the ford of Jabbok reveals the spiritual element in his nature. Reconstruct the scene for your hearers: Jacob and his family on the trek homeward, the goal of heart's desire ahead. Then comes the bad news. His brother, whom he had cheated, is waiting to get his own back. Jacob, still the wangler, sends gifts to the hate-filled brother and divides his caravan, sending his family into the disputed territory while he remains behind alone.

In the haunted darkness, Jacob broods and dreams. Conscience reasserts itself. Repressed decency and honor thrust themselves upward and forward in his soul, and the lower side of Jacob puts up a struggle. Then into this introspective hour and into Jacob's soul God breaks through. It was no ordinary man with whom Jacob wrestled. When a man comes morally and spiritually alive, he must struggle not only with the voices of his own past and of his own soul, but with the unseen Companion. All night the contest continued. The strange adversary asked to be released. Jacob's reply is one of the classic statements of the spiritual life: "I will not let thee go except thou bless me." And the other did bless Jacob — with a new name, Israel ("Striver-with-God") and with new insight and the beginnings of a new nature and way of life. Understandably Jacob named the scene of the divine-human encounter Penuel ("God's Face"), saying, "I have seen God face to face, and yet am alive!"

What may this story mean for modern strugglers? Its spiritual or psychological significance is relevant and could be transforming.

I. *Wrestling with ultimate questions*. Beyond solutions of immediate problems we must seek the answer to the ultimate questions: What is the nature of reality? What is God like? Be sure to ask these questions of the right person. If Jesus is the "Traveler unknown," stay with him until day breaks and you know that he that sees him sees the Father of all. "Tell me thy name, . . . for I will not let thee go except thou bless me."

> "Come, O thou Traveler unknown,
> Whom still I hold but cannot see;
> With thee all night I mean to stay,
> And wrestle till the break of day."

Someone listening to you may need that word to hold on a little longer. He whom we seek first of all seeks us.

II. *Wresting victory from disaster*. Because there is this other in our life, the most painful experience may yield permanent benefit. Men and women up against it, who, like Jacob, have held on until some blessing of increased strength or tenderness has come, signal this truth to those in deep trouble. Of course, the struggle may prove unequal. Before a dreaded antagonist a good soul may go down. But for the wrestler who has faith and faith's tenacity, the promise is sure. No one courts disaster. No one likes trouble. But when disaster or trouble comes, God's grace helps us to wrest victory from it. Recall some of the shining Christian examples: Robertson of Brighton, losing his chance of a military career to lead an army of Christ; Phillips Brooks, abjectly failing in his chosen profession of teaching, becoming a tremendously effective teacher of the truth in Christ; George Matheson, suffering blindness, but by his glorious faith and love lighting the way for spiritually sightless pilgrims; Studdert-Kennedy, putting up with asthma but assuring us between world wars that God has "the hardest part." There are so many gallant saints who,

> "Doomed to go in company with pain,
> And fear, and bloodshed, miserable train!,
> Turn [their] necessity to glorious gain;
> In face of these doth exercise a power
> Which is our human nature's highest dower;
> Controls them and subdues, transmutes, bereaves
> Of their bad influence, and their good receives."
>
> — *William Wordsworth*

Take Care of Yourself

This sounds like the solicitude of an overcautious parent or friend. Certainly "Take care," "So long," and "Be seeing you" have almost replaced "Good-by" ("God be with ye"). "Take care" even runs — in our region — a close second to "Take it easy." Admittedly the admonition can be sub-Christian. Life is found by those who throw it away for Christ's sake and the gospel's. When the self makes its health and welfare the top priority, the self itself deteriorates and may even disintegrate. But the essence of the Christian life is not self-annihilation.

Not long ago in a country church I sang a hymn which in its fourth stanza had us singing — not too heartily — "Make this poor self grow less and less." Is it right or Christian to pray for that progressive extinction of the personality God has given and whose growth is one of his chief concerns? Does not Christ say to every man and every woman, "Take care of your self"? Luke tells us that at their last supper together our Lord turned to Simon Peter and said in effect, "Simon, Simon, take care of yourself" (Luke 22:31-32). "I have prayed for you that you may not lose your faith. Yes, when you have turned back to me, you must strengthen these brothers of yours" (Phillips).

There is such a thing as Christian self-realization. "Thou shalt love thyself" can be more than indefensible egotism. The Christian importance of taking care of the self suggests that we may have a self worth investing in other selves and worth offering as a sacrifice to God (Rom. 12:1). How do you take Christian care of yourself?

Here are some directives:

I. *Find yourself* by knowing yourself as a child-of-God-in-the-making. One psychologist paraphrased Jesus' tremendous saying in this way: "He that loses his life on a lower level of development will find it on a higher level." I think I see something useful in that paraphrase.

II. *Deny yourself* in your individualistic demands for first place, for security, and for domination.

III. *Accept yourself* in your limitations, your weaknesses, and your strengths. In his autobiography, Prof. George Herbert Palmer, of Harvard, wrote: "Now it is foolish to sit lamenting over what one has not. The wisdom of life is to accept whatever comes and extract power from it." This was the man who in his youth was deeply discouraged about his life, for he was handicapped by physical weakness. His college president, Tucker of Dartmouth, advised him to ignore his defects and make himself spiritually robust enough "to carry them off." Dr. Palmer must have found power somewhere to do it; he lived creatively to the age of ninety-one.

IV. The final Christian wisdom is, *expose yourself* to the highest, which means to keep yourself constantly in Christ's company. Said Saint Augustine, "We are our loves." We become like that which we habitually admire. To practice His presence we must pray genuinely and often. We must keep our appointment with him in his house, at his Table, and on the work project in which he asks us to join.

An acquaintance twitted an old man who had been truly converted, "Well, Sam, I hear you've got the mastery of the devil." "No, sir," replied Sam, "but I've got the Master of the devil for my friend."

Christ enables us to reintegrate our lives with God's life-changing forces of love. We take care of ourselves when we put ourselves in the care and at the service of the Master of the death-dealing forces. Then we can help him to strengthen our companions.

Christ's Cure of Fear

There is no fear in love, but perfect love casts out fear. For fear has to do with punishment, and he who fears is not perfected in love. I JOHN 4: 18.

Let not your hearts be troubled; believe in God, believe also in me. In my Father's house are many rooms. . . . Peace I leave with you; my peace I give to you. . . . Let not your hearts be troubled, neither let them be afraid. JOHN 14: 1-2, 27.

Fear can be an angel of the Lord to protect and guard us. Fear can be a teacher, imparting wisdom and understanding. So education derives partly from fear of ignorance, scientific medicine from fear of disease, atomic research partly from fear of annihilation by another nation that is also engaged in research for the same reason.

But morbid fears work havoc on personality and accelerate, if not induce, actual illness and death. Anxiety is fear-thought in place of forethought. Jesus offered no superficial treatment. He expelled the demons of fear. This Christ still does. In ancient legend, Cholera announced that she would kill 5,000 persons in Baghdad. When the casualty list showed 10,000 deaths after her visit, she explained, "I killed 5,000; fear killed the others."

I. *Three aids in expelling fear:*

1. Face the fears as honestly and as bravely as you can. Drag them out into the light, label them, classify them. Do so in the presence of God. When you find that a small percentage of your fears have real foundation, you also find you can handle them. Help comes.

2. Live each day in a day-tight compartment. Two physicians prescribed this. The divine Physician said: " Sufficient unto the day is the evil thereof. Do not be anxious about tomorrow." The other was the late Sir William Osler, who, in his famous address to medical students, " A Way of Life," advocated practicing the wisdom of Jesus.

3. Do something about your fear immediately. When we fail to woo sleep because a window shade is flapping or a faucet dripping, we must get up and remedy it. So we must do with more important concerns that inspire anxiety or even fear. " This do and thou shalt live," emphasizes more than a slogan of a peace-of-mind cult. Our Lord, knowing the sinister forces closing in upon him, said, " Rise, let us be going." Come, let's face it and do what can be done.

II. *Christ's attack on fear*. Dr. Paul Tillich's Terry Lectures at Yale University provide both analysis and three main points. Anxiety, says Dr. Tillich, is due to: (1) A sense of meaninglessness. Many moderns see no purpose, no sense, no design, in existence. Life is a blot and blank for them; it is " full of sound and fury, signifying nothing." (2) A sense of guilt. Some psychiatrists think that nearly all mental illness has guilt feelings at the bottom of it. Accusing memories, a sense of unforgiven sin and the despair which it breeds, haunt more persons than laymen realize. (3) The fear of death. Tillich thinks that this is the most fruitful source of anxiety. Certainly our common glorification of the body after death occurs, our refusal to face the brute fact of physical death, and our softening of the stark Biblical words concerning this inevitable fact, support the view.

Christ meets this anxiety with " deep therapy." First, he asks us to believe in God. There is Another involved in this mysterious business. God lives, and he is holy, righteous Love. We encounter him in our actual situation. Secondly, believe in Christ, and the anxiety of guilt meets its master. God in Christ brings God's forgiveness to bear upon our guilt. He expels the devils who keep gnawing at our peace. He stills the storms not only on the sea but in our souls. But we must face the sins, repent of them, turn them over to Christ, and accept his pardon. We then know the release that comes from believing that, although unacceptable, we are accepted, restored to the family, admitted to the land of beginning again. Thirdly, our Lord assures us that this universe is our Father's house, that we live in one " room " now and that beyond the door of death are other rooms, abiding places, or "stations," on the pilgrimage. "This is life eternal," that we know God and Jesus Christ whom he has sent. And this life in Christ continues in the next phase of existence, and forever, for the one who commits his way to the Lord of life and death. We live in a guarded and guided universe. Courage, brave heart! The future is His also.

Good News for the Anxious

Throw the whole of your anxiety upon Him, because He cares for you.

I PETER 5:7 (WEYMOUTH).

Here exegesis is recommended. Remind your hearers that this little letter, proudly wearing Saint Peter's name, was written in a chaotic time. The prescription began with a directive: " Humble yourselves under the mighty hand of God." Then, to use the RSV, " Cast all your anxieties on him, for he cares about you."

This presupposes that you have the faith, that you are " in," and that you are practicing the faith by the help of the One whose gift it is.

How can we practice this faith? How can we make God's care demonstrably real to ourselves when tortured by fear-thought instead of girded by forethought? More than one competent Christian counselor suggests there are three practical rules we can follow.

I. *Limit your load of worries.* Distinguish legitimate anxieties from baseless ones. As you face them, inevitably some relate to the unforeseeable future, and the future belongs to God. Some of your anxieties fester around past events, and these are in God's hand too. If they concern moral failures, is he not ready to forgive? Has he not dealt with them? Has the God and Father of our Lord Jesus Christ not put them far from him, " as far as the east is from the west "? In his love you too can put them from you.

II. *Stagger the load*. Spread it and break it up, so that you can deal with each anxiety as a single foe, rather than as a battalion. Sufficient for the day is today's evil. Tomorrow will take care of itself. Jesus lived a crowded life, but his life was never hectic. He can help us to expel the unholy trinity of worry, flurry, and hurry. He lived one day at a time, one hour, one moment. To the immediate need or problem he gave his best, and left the rest to his Father, whose love and wisdom never fails. " If your life is too long and hard, break it apart! Break it into hours, minutes, seconds. A single moment is always manageable, no matter what burden it brings. . . . And each night God sends a sunset to shut us away from tomorrow's problems."

III. *Share your load*. This does not mean to unload it on another who may be already weighed down with his own burdens. It does not mean spineless evasion of one's own responsibility. But face it with another — a trusted friend, a minister — and always with God. " In every thing . . . let your requests be made known unto God " (Phil. 4: 6). Prayer is the intercommunication system whereby we cast our anxieties upon One who loves the burden. Believe the doctrine of the Holy Spirit and practice the presence of the living Christ. He stands beside, and goes before, not to lighten every burden but to increase our strength. To be anxious about nothing, be prayerful about everything.

Peace of God

You will phrase it differently. Yet before you have finished preaching on it, your hearers will know the tremendous difference between specious peace of mind and the profound peace of soul which comes from being hidden with Christ in God.

One student recently turned from his first-year class in Greek exegesis to preach a sermon on this theme from the salutation of Saint Paul to the Galatian Christians: " Grace be unto you and peace from God our Father and from the Lord Jesus Christ." His outline consisted of two main headings: " What is God's grace? "; " What is God's peace? "

Reference to commentaries will give you suggestive exegetical help and ideas in the exposition which you can assimilate and weave into your treatment. You will think, too, of the tremendous affirmation in Rom. 5:1: " We have peace with God through our Lord Jesus Christ." And, like the Welsh evangelist, you will finally say " in Christ's stead " to those whose hands may be outstretched in longing for this peace, even though they sit quietly in their pews, " Take it, man, take it! " Christ's peace was his last legacy before he went to the cross. And we can have it, but only on his wonderful but definite terms.

HOLY WEEK

From Palm Sunday to Easter more Protestants than ever before demonstrate a willingness to observe the seven days that shook the world. We are grateful for this concern with Christ's last week. You will have explored several possibilities, including the "Seven Last Words" and the events of each of the days in that sad and splendid week. Why not use Monday through Thursday as occasions for a series of doctrinal-devotional studies on the truth in our basic relationships?

"In the light of the cross" we could examine (1) our knowledge of God; (2) our estimate of man; (3) family and friendships; and (4) salvation. If the type of Good Friday service we have lends itself to preaching, a fifth sermon could deal with our redemption in the light of Christ's sacrifice, and the preceding sermon (4) could deal with the church, the community of the redeemed, or with the sacrament of the Lord's Supper on the traditional anniversary of its institution. Such a meditation, illuminating the deep meanings of the sacrament, would lead the preacher to say: "And now, being clean through the word he has spoken to us on his cross, let us receive in our hearts by faith the sacrament of Calvary: 'This is my body, given for you. This is my blood, shed for you.'"

PALM SUNDAY

As on this day Christ entered the city near which he was to suffer and die, it is a strange coronation that we witness, and a short-lived triumph. But throughout the Christian Era, preachers have seen in it the divine invasion of the kingdoms and cities of this world, the courage and compassion of the Lord, the parable and prophecy of that day when the kingdoms of this world shall become the kingdoms " of our God and of his Christ."

Christ's Entrance

One sermon subject is suggested by Mark's brief verse describing what Jesus did on the first day of his last week: " And Jesus entered into Jerusalem, and into the temple: and when he had looked round about upon all things, and now the eventide was come, he went out unto Bethany with the twelve " (Mark 11:11). (1) He rode into the nation's capital, a king. He enters into our city. What does he see? (2) He entered the church. He made a survey. He loved the church; he loves it still. How would he appraise our church today? How would he find us—his members? (3) He entered the home of his friends. And what he saw in church and state and family strengthened his will to save us all.

GOOD FRIDAY

On Preaching the Cross

As we prepare to witness through our sermons and services to the truth of "the greatest drama ever staged," it is salutary to remind ourselves of what we know. In our own pilgrimage and preparation certain directives are given:

1. Dwell much in personal meditation and devotion on the love which flames forth "from the foundation of the world" on Golgotha. In that inextinguishable blaze, our sin — our possessiveness, greed, pride, and all the other ugly accompaniments of our waywardness — can be consumed. If, like Pilgrim, we have found the burden of our sin and guilt loosed and rolled away, we can speak convincingly to others who are tempted to believe that the good news of unmerited forgiveness is too good to be true. Then, from firsthand experience, we will "speak of what we know."

2. Avoid oversentimentalizing the tremendous story on the one hand and an arid intellectualism or theological rigidity on the other. Too easily we treat the cosmic drama of God's action in Christ as we tend to treat a moving play in a theater or on television. We shed a tear or two and then go on our way unaltered in our attitudes and actions. Or, repelled by an individualistic, narrow, traditional piety, we carefully exclude or soften the inherent emotional appeal of the divine sacrifice.

3. Be more concerned with holding up before men the One who, being "lifted up," has power to draw them, than with upholding a particular theory of what was done there. Assuredly, if we are faithful exponents of the truth, we must "theologize," and

as clearly as we can. But men are saved, not by their theory of the atonement, but by the fact the theory seeks to interpret. Arthur James Balfour, a distinguished philosopher, said, "If the atonement were not too wide for our intellectual comprehension, it would be too narrow for our spiritual necessities." An able theologian, James Denney, of Scotland, once said to a congregation that, Protestant though he was, he wished he might hold up a crucifix before them and cry, "God loved like that!"

4. Let the "whole counsel of God" speak through the word of the cross. Men and women, boys and girls need to know that they have sinned and come short of God's demand; they need the glad assurance of his forgiveness. This need is primarily, profoundly personal, but it is more than judgment and mercy declared on individual wrongdoing. Is any wrongdoing ever solely individual? We must show our fellow sinners — honestly and courageously — that each of us is involved in the social evils which crucified our Lord. "I am part of the sin of war, of economic exploitation, of racial discrimination, or political corruption and ineptitude." Repentance, realized forgiveness, a "new creation," a "more excellent way" of human relationships, active participation in the redeemed community — all this must be declared. With the demands must be linked God's promises. With his promises must be declared the assurance of God's victory. For the symbol of our faith is not a crucifix, but a transfigured cross. In a sense he hangs and suffers there as the victim of man's iniquity; but in another, glorious, sense the cross is empty.

5. Preach Christ crucified and *risen*. The anniversary of the day of his dying is *Good* Friday because the third day came, and with it his glorious resurrection. We celebrate, not a martyrdom, but a divine sacrifice vindicated by the response of the universe whereby God raised him from the dead that he might live forevermore. A Protestant bishop who served in World War I told of two brothers serving together. One saw the other blown to bits by a hand grenade. When the action subsided, the survivor went into a dugout, took a sheet of note paper, and on it drew a sunrise and a cross, writing beneath it, "God is love." He pinned the

paper on a wall to remind him that God lives and that suffering and death are not meaningless. That simple Christian in the hell of war and personal bereavement sensed, as an early church father said, that Christ turns our sunsets into sunrise. Beyond the crucifixion is the resurrection. God has the last word. As Faber's hymn puts it,

> "Victory remains with love:
> Jesus, our Lord, is crucified!"

"That I may know him," said Paul, "and the power of his resurrection, and the fellowship of his sufferings" (Phil. 3: 10).

The Royal Pathway of the Cross

In the Canadian province of New Brunswick there is a road much visited and discussed by tourists. Its chief attraction consists of the apparently magnetic properties of that section of the terrain. On what appears to be a level stretch of highway, a halted car moves forward (or backward) as if drawn by some mysterious force. Actually the "pull" is an illusion, for the road is not level, but merely part of a hill whose slope is imperceptible. During Lent many travelers will move along a road that has a truly magnetic hill drawing them forward to the supreme sacrifice of history. The road is what a medieval saint called "The Royal Pathway of the Holy Cross." The hill is Calvary. On Ash Wednesday, the first day of Lent, Christians begin the annual journey in imagination, faith, and love along the road that our Lord took to his suffering and death and resurrection. Even those of us who do not "keep Lent" in any formal fashion increasingly value the rich opportunities that the season affords for meditation on the mighty acts of God in the life and death of Jesus Christ.

Why is it that the cross exerts such strange fascination upon men's minds and emotions? Why does this instrument of agonizing death lead the generations on? Here our words falter and fail. Here our most profound explanations prove inadequate.

Somehow the living God in all his love meets us in that Man upon the cross as nowhere else. Somehow on what Bunyan called "that little place ascending" we know, to use the memorable words of a learned and acute Christian thinker of our time (Rosenstock-Huessy), that man is a loved soul. In what happened there once and for all, and happens again as we confront it and respond to it with loving acceptance, we who have no hope in ourselves are given hope. God, in whom we may have believed vaguely, becomes real, commanding, and transforming. We know that he must love the world to die for it, that he "loved me and gave himself for me," and for all men. Further, such love impels us to be cross-bearers, for

> "Love so amazing, so divine,
> Demands my soul, my life, my all."

The cross of Christ is the center and core of creation, the key to the riddle of life, and the divine law by which we must live. Having said this, we have said little to explain the power of the cross.

A story suggests what hosts of men and women know to be true. One day in the heart of London, a "bobbie" found a small boy crying his heart out. "What's the matter, my boy? Can I help you?" asked the policeman. "Oh," said the child, "I am lost." "Well, don't cry. We can fix that. Where do you live?" "If you will take me to the hill where the white cross stands, I can find my way," answered the lad. Lenten Sundays and Holy Week provide singularly effective times in which to take our people to "the hill where the white cross stands." For it is the one fixed signpost from which God's children of every sort, age, and condition can find their way home. Begin with the wounds of Christ, urged Luther. If we do not, can we, or those who look to us for help, ever hope to understand Christ or his gospel? In a sense deeper than many have thought, the gospel hymn expressed the truth: "The way of the cross leads home."

The One Sure Signpost

Twenty-nine years ago a woman novelist named Mary Webb died in her native England. Her fame has grown chiefly since her death. You may have read one of her somber and passionate novels of the Shropshire countryside which she loved intensely. In her first novel, *The Golden Arrow* (1916), there is a parable that is relevant to the season of Lent.

Deborah Arden, the heroine, is pictured standing on the heath and looking up at an old signpost. The author writes:

"The signpost looked, with its outspread arms against the dim reaches of the heather, like a crucifix under the troubled sky. It stood with forlorn gallantry between the coming storm and its prey. It would be lashed by rain all night; lightning would play around it. . . . Deborah, looking at it, wondered if she would ever be lonesome as it was, set up for sign, a mark for the storm pointing vaguely whither?"

To many of our contemporaries the church resembles that old signpost. They are glad to see it as a kind of familiar, reassuring landmark. They may not use it, certainly not to give them needed direction to take the right road to the city of God. But when the church uplifts the cross, and Him who made the cross the symbol of God's redemptive love, many modern pilgrims stand like Deborah Arden, gazing at it, wondering if it is indeed the one sure signpost. Does every man's soul, seeking a refuge from the coming storm, look hopefully to where the cross points? When the seeker looks at this ancient signpost, is the writing too faded to read? Wrote a Christian editor:

"The prodigal, at the end of his tether, has haunting memories of his long-forgotten home, and remembers the old road over the hill. But he has lost his way, and as he gazes at the cross, looking for some direction, he wants someone to help him to decipher the faded writing which might guide him homeward."

What do you mean by "homeward"? And who will decipher the writing? "Home" is in God. Remember Isaac Watts's grand paraphrase of Ps. 90:

" Our God, our Help in ages past,
Our Hope for years to come,
Our Shelter from the stormy blast,
And our eternal Home."

Who is the interpreter? Christ's messenger, the herald of the good news, the preacher! And the writing? Christians of all theological backgrounds agree that its core is John 3:16—and v. 17 too. We may differ as to the interpretation and application of the message—some prefer Saint Paul's or Paul Tillich's version—but the signpost of the cross points to the heart of God, to his self-giving in the divine Son of his love. It is " beneath the cross of Jesus " that we know we are loved creatures, accepted when we are unacceptable, and called to unlimited trust in God and unlimited self-giving to others in the grace of Christ.

The Bridge to God

From the Celtic twilight of ancient Wales comes this legend. In far-off days the warriors of the land were rushing through the wilderness to defend their homes and win peace and security. Suddenly they reached a raging river, across which they were powerless to go. There was no bridge, and to ford the angry waters was impossible. In this time of desperate need came one of the guardian giants of the Welsh. He laid down his great body across the torrent, and over him the men walked to safety and to the land where they would be. Afterward the giant was heard to say, " He who would lead the people must be a bridge."

Somehow, whatever our theology of the atonement, we think of the cross of Calvary as a bridge across which the imperiled pilgrims of nineteen centuries have moved, not only into safety, but into what the New Testament calls " newness of life," into victory over the worst that evil and time and death can do. The Lord Jesus Christ who laid his body on the tree was and is the " Pontifex Maximus," the chief bridge builder of the ages. By his perfect obedience to God's will, by his voluntary sacrifice of himself on Golgotha, the chasm between man and God, between time and eternity, has been bridged. Words fail, our most thoughtfully prepared explanations falter and collapse, but we know that through what God did in Christ on that gibbet outside Jerusalem centuries ago, we get " through " to the divine love and forgiveness. More important, we know that God " gets through " to us.

We need what the church has called atonement. We need to be, and in our sane hours want to be, reconciled to God. Do any of us doubt that because Jesus died a completely human death, voluntarily, we are restored to that fellowship with God which we and all men were made for, and which we threw away by our own folly? Is not this bridging the abyss of separation and of alienation what Paul means when he speaks of salvation as " reconciliation "? Look up the relevant passages where this concept is used (Rom. 5: 10 f.; II Cor. 5: 18-20; Eph. 2: 16; Col. 1: 20 ff.). Our Biblical theologians confirm our impression that the basic idea is of restoration to fellowship with God. And we need it, and we need to tell our people in these days leading to Easter that they need it too.

Dr. A. M. Hunter, the popular and scholarly Aberdeen teacher, in his book *Interpreting Paul's Gospel,* which comprised his lectures at Union Theological Seminary, Richmond, Virginia, offered a wonderfully clear discussion of the main points of the New Testament faith. Professor Hunter says that when Paul uses the term " reconciliation " for salvation, it is his best way of putting it, " because it lifts the whole issue from the level of the law court to the plane of personal relations; because, too, the hunger for reconciliation with reality — however it be conceived — is something elemental and universal. . . . Man's need is to recover the lost fellowship, to be restored to the family circle, to get out of disgrace into grace." And only God can do that, and God has done it and is doing it and will do it until God sees the travail of man's soul and is satisfied that all is complete.

Doesn't the thought of it make you want to preach from " deep down " at the center of the faith in Holy Week? Could you not try to make clear what the meanings of the cross are? With recoveries of the central message of the faith going on all over Christendom, and with the human situation being what it is, we shall never "traffic in pale and pithless platitudes" about the cross and resurrection. For never is the cross to be fully understood, nor preached, apart from its mighty and mysterious sequel.

> "When the hymnodist asked the saints
> Whence their victory came,
> They, with united breath,
> Ascribed their conquest to the Lamb,
> Their triumph to his death."

But it was the death of One who could not be held by death, One in whose death death itself was slain. As we plan our preaching for Holy Week, we shall think chiefly of Palm Sunday and Easter. We do well to think of the Sundays after Easter as opportunities to continue our proclamation of the good news as it centers in the death and resurrection of our Lord.

Characters in the Greatest Drama

A series on the cross which has appealed to many portrays "The Characters in the Greatest Drama." In one Lenten season I announced a series with titles such as:

"The Churchmen"
"The Governor"
"The Informer" (Judas Iscariot)
"The Sailor Afraid of the Sea" (Simon Peter)
"The Crowd"
"Public Enemy Number One"
"The Victim Who Became Victor"

You will think of others, such as Joseph of Arimathaea, the mysterious fugitive (John Mark, who fled the soldiers who arrested Jesus), the women who stood by the cross, the soldiers, "they that passed by." To the meager yet meaningful clues to their character and action furnished by the Gospels, you will add legendary material, and draw on your own reverent imagination. Such portraits can be drawn vividly, and both instruction and evangelism will result.

A series of Lenten sermons could follow: " What They Said at Calvary " or " Words and Actions During the Supreme Tragedy." A simpler, more direct general title for such a series might be " Words at the Cross ": (1) What the Governor Said (John 19: 22). (2) What the Important People Said (Matt. 27: 12-13 and parallel passages in other Gospels). (3) What the Spectators Said (Matt. 27: 39-40, 47, 49). (4) What the Church Leaders Said (Matt. 27: 41-43). (5) What the Condemned Criminals Said (Luke 23: 39-42). (6) What the Army Officer Said (Mark 15: 39). (7) What the Crucified Said (Matt. 27: 46; Mark 15: 34; Luke 23: 34, 43, 46; John 19: 26-28, 30).

The Cross Today

A brief series on " The Cross Today " could have for titles: " Around the Cross," " Over the Cross," and " Beneath the Cross." For the first, these texts suggest themselves: Luke 23: 35-36, 47, 49. In this sermon you could deal with the groups who watched him die and who directly or indirectly contributed to his death. " There they crucified him." Who is meant? (1) The crowd — " The people stood by, watching " — persons whom he loved, believed in, and helped. (2) " The rulers scoffed at him." Loyal churchman, trusted leaders, respectable citizens — the " best people " — were among the rulers, and still are. (3) " The soldiers also mocked him." Not all soldiers did then, or do now, but military life " depersonalizes " men. (4) " And all his acquaintances and the women who had followed him." They loved him, and their love cast out fear, if not their deep sorrow.

For the second sermon, " Over the Cross," the Scriptural basis is John 19: 19-22. Here you could make a character study of Pilate. Use the danger signals flashed to him during his encounter with the Prisoner who gave the Roman governor an immortality of infamy. What were these " signals "? (1) The voice of conscience demanding justice. (2) The voice of superhuman goodness, of holiness, of mysterious " otherness " in Christ, inspiring awe, respect, fear. (3) The voice of love, the warning from Pilate's wife. And then Pilate wrote the inscription for the cross. Whether Pilate's writing was intended to infuriate or to placate the Jews, or expressed a grudging acknowledgment of the kingliness of the crucified, we may not know. We do know that it was truer than Pilate or the others could have dreamed: Jesus is the King of all the world, and of his Kingdom there shall be no end. Do we acknowledge his right to reign, in our lives, our community, our nation, and our world?

"Beneath the Cross" includes "Simon, a Cyrenian," who was passing by (Mark 15:21). An introduction might quickly answer the questions: Who was Simon? Why was he chosen? Could something like his experience happen to us? Go downtown one day on a perfectly reasonable bit of business and encounter Christ and the claims of his cross, and your life is forever different. You become a conscript of the cross. Then you help your people to look at Simon beneath the cross—and themselves sharing Christ's burden. It may be the result of a chance meeting. Decisive as it later proves, it may be—usually is—unwelcome at the time. But, as one said of Moses, so we may be "frustrated into sublimity." For all noble living begins with the acceptance of the cross, and is centered in Christ's love forever after.

Words from the Cross

Six Sundays are available in Lent, and on them you may wish to take as many "words from the cross." If you prefer taking "the seven words," there is no reason why you should not begin with the Sunday preceding the first in Lent. In the seventh century the forty days of Lent were lengthened by designating three pre-Lenten Sundays.

Even if you participate in a three-hour Good Friday service, you may find it rewarding to base six or seven sermons on the words reported by the four Gospel writers to have been uttered by the dying Savior. Brooding over the Evangelists' record of his last hours in the light of all that they mean to you, and could mean to modern "lives of quiet desperation," will make you creative in your preaching. Here are themes which you may wish to phrase in your own way:

"Forgiveness, Human and Divine"
"What Death Could Mean"
"Christ Taught Us to Care"
"Black Despair and the Way Through"
"Christ and Our Elemental Needs"
"What Calvary Completed"
"The Victory of the Cross"

Affirmations of the Cross

Someone has observed that the only route from Palm Sunday to Easter Sunday runs straight through the desolation of Good Friday. This is why that which the church calls Holy Week is at once the most dreadful and the most blessed week of all history. On Good Friday we rightly glory in the cross, join Saint Paul in resolving to know only Christ and him crucified (I Cor. 2:2). But when Paul thus spoke it is unlikely that he concentrated at all on the physical pain of Jesus' crucifixion, for not in its horror lies the power of the cross. To be preoccupied with the details of the "agony and bloody sweat" would impress the apostle as perversion of the gospel of the cross. While no one should forget what was done to our Lord by men, the significance of the cross lies in what Jesus did. All that he asked to save the world was a cross whereon to die, said a saint. Why Paul turned again and again to the cross, made it central in his message, was that it was "the instrument of the amazing act of love and self-giving which sets men free." This is the mood, the emphasis, that should dominate our Good Friday preaching.

We see Jesus on the cross, the eternal Judge of all the powers of evil, and the eternal Savior of men. To be saved, we must confront this heartbreaking truth by which we are judged and condemned, but we must always realize that it is the judgment and the condemnation of holy love. And no sooner have we heard the verdict than we feel a divine hand lifting us up. He is our Judge and our Savior. "Note then the kindness and the severity of God."

Is there not a sermon here? Why not take the two tremendous affirmations that focus this truth: "Now is the judgment of this world, now shall the ruler of this world be cast out; and I, when I am lifted up from the earth, will draw all men to myself" (John 12: 31-32), and, "Far be it from me to glory except in the cross of our Lord Jesus Christ, by which the world has been crucified to me, and I to the world" (Gal. 6: 14). One obvious plan for such a sermon would answer certain questions: Why is the cross the focal point of the Christian message? Why do we glory in it? How does the Crucified judge and save us?

Dialogue at the Cross

There was a dialogue at the cross when Jesus of Nazareth died on it. There has been a dialogue at the cross ever since.

I. *There was a dialogue, a debate, among the soldiers of the execution squad.* Not all were interested, but some were (Matt. 27: 35). Soldiers ask questions, argue, speculate. Their subject on that black day would be the condemned. Their questions: What's the score? Is this what comes to a man of faith and goodness? Where is God? Yet, all the time, Another was speaking to them through Christ. This is the key to the riddle of life. Here is the secret of great living. And the Other awaited their response.

II. *There was a dialogue between sensitive souls, confronting the suffering of the innocent.* "There were also many women there, looking on from afar, who had followed Jesus from Galilee, ministering to him" (Matt. 27: 55). What is the use of such suffering? Can God be Love and yet permit this cruelty? And all the time God was answering, speaking through the Suffering Servant of Calvary. No easy and complete solutions to the problem were given. But something better is apparent. There is no life except through death, no gain except through loss, no crown without the cross. And for us and our dear ones who suffer, the

New Testament insight comes: "The pain God is allowed to guide ends in a saving repentance never to be regretted, whereas the world's pain ends in death" (II Cor. 7:10, Moffatt). Intellectuals cannot help much, but the saints get through deep waters quite easily.

III. *At Golgotha there was the dialogue between the two thieves and Jesus* (Luke 28:40). Is there forgiveness for the worst sinner? It was no one-way conversation. God heard and answered in Christ: "Today shalt thou be with me." The cross is the door through which the Father welcomes the penitent prodigal back to the family, and home!

> "I know not how that Calvary's cross
> A world from sin could free;
> I only know its matchless love
> Has brought God's love to me."

IV. *Most revealing of all was the dialogue between Christ and his Father.* The Gospels report one side of it: "Father, forgive them." "My God, why?" "Father, into thy hands." Was there response? We are here and have the grace wherein we stand because God answered. The answer was the resurrection. And ever since men have known that he is the Victor. "Remember Jesus Christ, risen."

Still the dialogue proceeds. Now it is between the soul and God. Across the same sharp issues it continues: What is life's meaning? Why do the innocent suffer? How can we be forgiven? Will love and goodness and truth ever win? We must listen for God's answer. And we cannot hear and know unless we respond to what he has spoken and done in the life and death and victory of the Son of his love. Our response is the decision of our lives. On the answer we give depends the reply that comes back from him.

Dimensions of the Cross

On the threshold of his tragedy and triumph a sermon on the cross may be preached using the dimensions of the cross symbolically. Moffatt's translation of Gal. 3:1 is a dramatic, gripping indictment: "You who had Jesus Christ the crucified placarded before your very eyes." Even in a secularized culture it remains true. What does it signify? Are we also "bewitched," as were the Galatian Christians Paul rebuked? Graphically this sermon would recall: (1) The cross points upward—high as heaven. (2) It goes straight down into the earth, deep as hell, the hell of our sin, and as deep as the grave. The good news of the cross gives deep treatment to our sin and overcomes the sharpness of death. (3) The arms of the cross are outstretched to enfold the world. Only the twisted cross can symbolize exclusiveness. (4) The cross is a signpost, giving us direction, an instrument of communication.

> "Near the cross I'll watch and wait,
> Hoping, trusting ever,
> Till I reach the golden strand
> Just beyond the river.
> —*Fanny J. Crosby*

A Trilogy on the Cross

A trilogy of studies of Christ and his cross attempts to clarify some of the meanings of the cross: What did it mean for Christ? for God? for us? Years ago, the late George H. Morrison, of Wellington Church, Glasgow, Scotland, published a striking little book on these questions. Long before Dr. Peter Marshall made the staccato style and format of sermons popular, Dr. Morrison used it in this particular study. Others may have published sermonic treatments of the same pivotal questions. But you and I should give our answers, and help others to saving insights into the significance of history's crucial action.

V

EASTERTIDE

Season of the Resurrection

EASTER

Of course, every Sunday is Resurrection Day. To the man of faith it is so because of what happened on the first Easter. Few preachers need to be recalled to the central emphasis in Easter preaching. While the gospel brought life and immortality to light, Easter is more than a festival of immortality. It is a day of eternal hope. Because he lives, we too shall live who are " in Christ." But supremely Easter celebrates the victory of God in Christ over sin and death and time.

If you have preached Easter sermons for five, ten, a dozen, or more years to the same congregation, you may find yourself biting the end of your pen in a vain hope of inspiration if not sustenance! Fret not that variations on the same theme will be unwelcome.

The Easter Key

Remember Jesus Christ, risen from the dead.

II TIMOTHY 2:8.

The key to all our love and hope,
All our joy and kindness
All our forgiveness and faith
Was found nineteen hundred years ago
On the top of a lonely hill.

— *Barbara Harbert*

It would not have been found on that hill if what happened there had been the end of Jesus. But, as Peter declared, " This

Jesus God raised up, and of that we are all witnesses" (Acts 2:32). Christianity's tremendous claim is that the action of God in raising Jesus Christ from the dead is the master key which opens the doors shut and locked by evil and death. "Take this key," says the Spirit speaking through the church and to the churches. "You will find it opening doors into fullness of life, love, hope, and victory."

I. *The resurrection fact opens the door marked "Life's Meaning."* Sentimentally we sing, "Ah, sweet mystery of life!" But life's mystery can be anything but sweet; it can be bitter with disillusionment, unpalatable, and revolting. God in Christ, God who disclosed "his own purpose . . . now has manifested [this purpose, this meaning] through the appearing of our Savior Jesus Christ, who abolished death and brought life and immortality to light" (II Tim. 2:9-10). The risen Christ is the meaning of life. Holy, righteous love is operating here, and as we respond to this love, we see that life is no blot or blank for us, but that it means good. We find a pattern in existence, make sense of it, and are convinced that "all things work together" according to his plan. Our little lives, with their tragedy and gains, are his concern, and we matter to him more than wheeling systems do. Not the stars, but souls are his most valued possessions. As we love Him who first loved us and demonstrated his love by the life, death, and resurrection of his Son, Jesus, and as we love our neighbor with something of his love, life ceases to be an enigma and becomes eternally significant.

II. *The Risen Lord conquered evil.* The powers of darkness and the demonic forces in the world and in us were vanquished. His first followers claimed that this Galilean carpenter and teacher was Lord over all things, forever. Absurd, incredible claim! Yet they went out in the power of the resurrection to substantiate that claim. Their exploits from the first Christian century to this can be explained on no other basis than that of their complete confidence that Christ had risen from the dead, had defeated the militant, organized powers of evil, and had commissioned them to take every man, every community, every nation captive for him. When you despair concerning the world, " remember Jesus Christ, risen," who must reign until all the kingdoms of this world become his Empire of love. The Easter key unlocks the prison house where evil thrusts its victims.

III. *The Easter key opens the door of the tomb.* Christ broke through the most impregnable fortress that awaits the human personality, death. On the resurrection morning, he not only broke through; he abolished death completely, " and has now, through the Gospel, opened to us men the shining possibilities of the life that is eternal " (II Tim. 1: 10, Phillips). The key unlocks the door through which so many are afraid to pass, at which so many contemporaries are even afraid to look. Those who are " in Christ " through loving trust and membership in his body, the redemptive community of Christ, shall know. " The saying is sure: If we have died with him, we shall also live with him; if we endure, we shall also reign with him " (II Tim. 2: 11-12). " I have the keys," John heard the glorified Redeemer of the apocalypse say. He is the key. The risen Master is the Master Key. " Fear not. Because I live, ye shall live also. Behold I was dead and am alive again. I have the keys of death and hell."

Easter means only an interlude in the world's miseries, a breathing space in the mad rush of fearsome days, a wistful hope of broken hearts — unless you have the key, unless you let Him who is himself the key open the gates of new life for you. " See the Christ stand! "

The Easter Revolution

No, not any twentieth-century political upheaval, but something infinitely more significant, is reported in John 20: 14, 16: " And . . . she turned herself back, and saw Jesus standing." (1) It was a revolution in Mary's conception of her Master. Easter still works a revolution in men's thoughts of God and Christ. The revelation induces a revolution in our views of reality. (2) The first Easter turned the disciples' little community upside down.

What had been a small secret society became the holy catholic church. (3) The Easter revolution transforms our attitude toward death. Physical death cannot sever our most precious relationships.

Invincible Assurance

" But now is Christ risen from the dead " (I Cor. 15: 20) and " I know whom I have believed, and am persuaded that he is able to keep that which I have committed unto him against that day " (II Tim. 1: 12). Here is our tremendous certitude. Of what are we assured? Of God's unfailing care, that the best rises victorious out of the worst, that death is conquered.

> " When the anxious hearts say, 'Where? '
> He doth answer, 'In my care.'
> " 'Savior, tell us, where are they? '
> 'In my keeping, night and day.'
> " 'Tell us, tell us how it stands.'
> 'None shall pluck them from my hands.' "

The Easter Secret

Death had no more dominion over him.

ROMANS 6: 9.

Etch in the two pictures of the disciples, before and after the Event. Indicate how the secret communicates assurance and victory for us today concerning our beloved in the unseen and concerning the future of the great cause of Christ's Kingdom.

Resurrection Now!

The hour is coming, and now is, when the dead will hear the voice of the Son of God, and those who hear will live.

JOHN 5: 25, 28.

It can happen to us here, and now!

Point out the use of the present tense in New Testament references: "This *is* eternal life . . . He who has the Son has life," and others. Tell the people how Christ can bring them out of the tombs of deadening habit, of broken hopes, and of killing sorrow. "Easter begins, like all deep things, in mystery, and it ends, like all high things, in a great courage."

The Three Resurrections

This fruitful theme was suggested, I think, by Dr. Boynton Merrill, of Columbus, Ohio. Three texts could be Mark 16:6, "He has risen"; John 20:20, "The disciples were glad when they saw the Lord"; and Rom. 6:4, 11, "So that as Christ was raised up from the dead by the glory of the Father, we too might walk in newness of life. . . . So you also must consider yourselves dead to sin and alive to God in Christ Jesus."

Resurrection one: the resurrection of Jesus Christ. Resurrection two: that of the disciples, the resurrection *in* the disciples. Resurrection three: that resurrection which should and can occur in us. Millions now living are already dead; they live as if Easter were only an affair of sentimental hopes, Easter bunnies, eggs, and flowers. Expose yourself to the divine power, the living Lord of life and history. He is experienced first as an Influence, afterward as a Light, and at last and forever after as a Presence.

Life Begins at Easter

The Christian celebrates Easter fifty-two times a year. Every Sunday is the Day of the Lord. This familiar story was told of Dr. R. W. Dale, famous British preacher of the last century. When a visitor to his church one November morning heard the hymn, "Christ is risen: Hallelujah!" he expressed his surprise to the preacher. "I want my people to know the glorious fact that Christ is alive and to rejoice over it, and Sunday is the day on which he rose," explained Dr. Dale. But Easter Day superlatively is the occasion to proclaim this radiant truth of our faith. "At the first signs of dawn on the first day of the week, they went to the tomb" (Luke 24:1, Phillips), prepared for a funeral, and were confronted by a resurrection. God raised Jesus Christ from the dead, and as one after another of the other lights of human wisdom fail, Christ stands out — as a rebel prophet of the Roman Catholic Church, Father Tyrrell, said — luminous against the prevailing light.

This victory of God in our risen Lord we proclaim. Easter is not a festival of immortality, but the anniversary of God's mighty act whereby Christ became Victor. Christian thinkers are right when they assert that the immortality of the soul — if by it is meant a kind of immortal soul-substance in every man — is not a Christian doctrine. Although the Bible speaks of immortality, its chief concern is not the continuity of individual organisms, but of the personal relationship between God and men. Biblical basis for belief in immortality is more than confidence in the everlasting quality of the human soul; its foundation is that "life in God, and especially in the risen Christ, cannot cease."

"We look at it like this," writes Paul in II Cor. 5:14 ff.: "If One died for all men then, in a sense, they all died, and His purpose in dying for them is that their lives now should be no longer lived for themselves but for Him Who died and rose again for them. . . . For if a man is in Christ he becomes a new person altogether — the past is finished and gone, everything has become fresh and new. All this is God's doing, for He has reconciled us to Himself through Jesus Christ; and He has made us agents of the reconciliation" (Phillips).

Post-mortem Influence or Personal Presence?

This query is not commended as a sermon title, but it is set down starkly to stab our minds awake as to the issue of Easter. Dr. Albert Schweitzer once said that Paul grasped the fact that the essence of being a Christian lies in the experience of being in fellowship with Christ. But this fellowship is not merely imaginative, posthumous, or completely spiritualized. "Now *is* Christ risen from the dead." He is, as the Roman soldier in Masefield's drama said, "let loose in the world." Men and women meet him today "in spite of death." The New Testament Christians never remembered Christ. To them he was a present companion. Said James S. Stewart, "Look at the sequence, risen from the dead, therefore alive forever, therefore our contemporary, therefore able to confront us face to face" (*A Faith to Proclaim*).

Christianity is no exercise for antiquarians. It is communion with the divine Contemporary. Why not take as a text one of the tremendous affirmations where the present tense of the risen Lord is used? Consider II Cor. 2:14: "Thanks be to God, who in Christ always leads us in triumph." As Christ died and rose, so the believer in him dies and rises into the new, victorious, and eternal life. Here are certain striking propositions which I owe to our Ceylonese leader of the world church, Dr. Daniel T. Niles: (1) To live in a world where Christ is risen is to live in a world where Christ is our contemporary. (2) To live in a world where Jesus is risen is to live in a world where Jesus is Lord (Matt. 11:27). (3) To live in a world where Jesus is risen is to live in a world in which Jesus is inescapable. (4) To live in a world where Jesus is risen is to live in a world where Jesus is at work.

To preach the resurrection rather than a vague belief in immortality is to invite men and women to an encounter with the risen and reigning Lord of life and history. To do so as faithfully as in us lies may be to reproduce something of the apostolic success recorded in Acts 4:33: "And with great power the apostles gave their testimony to the resurrection of the Lord Jesus, and great grace was upon them all."

FIRST SUNDAY AFTER EASTER

Exile's Return

The first Sunday after Easter is designated by our more liturgically minded brethren as "Low Sunday." Attendance commonly ebbs after the apex of the Christian year has been reached.

Have you preached on the sequel to the first Easter, so dramatically reported in John 20:19-29? Here is a superb field to work over for an expository sermon. Expository preaching, like the classics, is praised by many. Some assume that a recovery of it would solve all questions raised by criticism of much current pulpit work. Agreed, it is one of the most effective, as it is one of the most exacting, types of preaching. Its virtues do not make other kinds of sermons obsolete or necessarily superficial. Nevertheless, one convincing argument for expository preaching was advanced by the late Principal John Oman, of Westminster College, Cambridge, England: "Until you select preachers like poultry on the principle of laying all the year round, you can hardly expect them to produce out of their own inward experience a perpetual stream of sermons with the germ of life in them." Therefore, he counseled, expound passages of Scripture, and transmit the insights born of the experience of others who were manifestly God's agents and instruments. We too would agree that exposition of the Scriptures would be a welcome novelty in many pulpits.

To proceed with a sermon for the Sunday following Easter, let your imagination play on persons and events of "the evening of that day, the first day of the week," when the disciples met behind closed doors "for fear." Of course, the man who has an evening preaching service on Easter Day has an advantage. The Gospel narrative synchronizes with Easter Sunday evening perfectly. But for others also the passage is timely.

"Now Thomas, one of the twelve, called the Twin, was not with them when Jesus came. . . . Eight days later [just over a week], his disciples were again in the house, and Thomas was with them. The doors were shut [again], but Jesus came and stood among them, and said, 'Peace be with you'" (John 20:24, 26).

I. *Introduction.* "Thomas . . . was not with them when Jesus came." He should have been. It was the evening of the first Christian Sunday, the day that changed the face of the world. His friends must have told him of the meeting in the Chapel of the Presence which we know as the upper room. He must have known of the tremendous event of that wonderful morning. But "Thomas . . . was not with them when Jesus came." He had exiled himself from the homeland of faith. By his own edict he had excommunicated his spirit from the fellowship.

II. *Body of the Sermon.* Why did he do it? He was no deserter, no timid rabbit. "Let us also go, that we may die with him" (John 11:16), he had said when his Lord resolved to risk his life on an errand of mercy. Was it because now, after the black tragedy of the Friday, he was Despairing Thomas even more than Doubting Thomas? When his comrades tried repeatedly to reassure him that his beloved Chief had visited them after his death, he was incredulous, perhaps sullen. "You don't catch me believing in ghosts."

Where was he? Doing something useful, probably. But, Thomas, you should have been in the upper room. You needed that fellowship and the others needed you.

1. Modern Thomas — living with frustration, bitter disappointment; disillusioned by events, personal and global; lonely, anxious — needs the upper room. Worship week by week is no luxury, but an imperative necessity. In our upper room we need to

meet with him and with his friends.

2. What may we find? What Thomas found when he did return from his exile — the living Lord Jesus Christ. In such contact power is released: power for cleansing, for renewal for problem-solving, for living the life that is life indeed. If you see Thomas this week, tell him what he missed. Tell him what he is missing when he forsakes the rendezvous with God.

III. *Conclusion.* For the returning exile, Christ's crowning beatitude is reserved: " Blessed are those who have not seen and yet believe " (John 20: 29). " Happy are the men who have never seen me and yet believe." Faith is not sight, but insight. We mature, become adequate for every testing, as we endure " as seeing him who is invisible." Would you know that God is, and that he is Love, your Savior and Guide? Keep your appointment with the fellowship. He is known where two or three, or two or three hundred or thousand, meet together in his name and in his spirit. He is known by all who worship him and by all who go forth from worship to serve in his spirit and in his cause.

An ancient legend tells of Thomas' going with Bartholomew to India in fulfillment of the Great Commission, and there baptizing into the faith the three Wise Men who came to Bethlehem years before. Whatever Thomas' subsequent life became, it would be one of usefulness and meaning. Contact with the risen Lord was all that he needed to inspire and equip him. It is all that you and I need. " Whom having not seen, ye love; in whom, though now ye see him not, yet believing, ye rejoice with joy unspeakable and full of glory " (I Peter 1: 8).

" O strangely art thou with us, Lord,
Neither in height nor depth to seek;
In nearness shall thy voice be heard;
Spirit to spirit thou dost speak."

The Easter Sequel

You reconstruct the scene of John, ch. 20. The disciples meet behind closed doors, afraid, and then the miracle of the Presence:

" Jesus came and stood among them and said to them, ' Peace be with you.' " Luke tells us the disciples were terrified. Was this a radically different appearance of the risen Lord from the other appearances on that greatest of all days? " When he had said this," as if to reassure them beyond any doubt or qualm, " he showed them his hands and side." That did it; this was their dear Lord, the Jesus of the scars: " Then the disciples were glad when they saw the Lord." Again he repeated his greeting: " Peace be with you." It was a customary salutation of the East.

But a great soul charges a conventional word with new meaning and power. Peace had been almost his last word before he went to the agony of the Garden, the trial, and the crucifixion. Now he gives them his peace. He fulfills his earlier promise. This is not the peace of passivity, of psychological autosuggestion, of soporifics and sedatives, verbal or otherwise. Then immediately he issues his directive: " As the Father has sent me, even so I send you." It recalls the Great Commission which is the warrant for all the missionary and evangelistic activity of the Church across the centuries. It is the only invariable element in all the resurrection narratives. This commission has never been revoked.

Could you not expound this Scripture so that men would know that Christ's peace is available, adequate, and to be found, not in rest from labor, but in rest in toil for his cause? Once I used this passage in a sermon on the first Sunday after Easter when I presented an appeal for a new forward movement in the church. I recalled an old preacher's division of Paul's exclamation when faced with adversities which would have defeated lesser men: " None of these things move me." " Brethren," said the preacher, " I will divide my sermon under three heads: First, some things should move us. Secondly, some things should not move us. Thirdly, we should move some things." Christ's victory and his marching orders should move us. The apathy and resistance of people to causes needing assistance should not move us. We should move the weight of responsibility which is ours as Christ's people by getting under it ourselves. If you have not used it, the illustration used by Dr. Leslie D. Weatherhead during World War II may be useful. It is indicated when you anticipate the rationalization good people still make when they oppose expenditure of money and time on "foreign" missions. In Hyde Park, London, a listener tried to heckle a Christian preacher by shouting: "Christianity has been in the world for two thousand years and look at the state of the world!" Back came the retort: "Yes, and water has been in the world for two billion years, and look at the state of your face!" It points to one part of the answer. Dreadful conditions still prevailing these nineteen hundred years after Christ's advent and resurrection argue for the necessity of a far more dynamic and universal Christian campaign rather than for the futility of it.

After a message of this character, it is not difficult to pray: "Eternal God, whose Son lives to redeem and lead thy children, grant us grace not only to worship him as our risen Savior, but to obey him as our divine Lord and Leader. Teach us that until we know the sacrifices for thy Kingdom we cannot know the peace of Christ which passes understanding. Go with us as we go upon thy business, in Jesus Christ, thy Son, our Lord."

RURAL LIFE SUNDAY

What to Do with Weeds

Let both grow together until the harvest.

MATTHEW 13:30.

That infernal, ubiquitous weed! In any month of growing, how it thrives! If, as is the case with New Englanders, you can count on a rich crop of crab grass, you know the feeling. Here are the "tares" of evil in the field of the world. Is there any wisdom about handling the problem? (1) The Master faces the fact honestly. Evil exists. He gives no intellectual solution to the enigma. An enemy has done this. And with this foe there can be no truce. (2) What shall we do with the evil now that we recognize it?

Pick it out and destroy it? Gardeners are ruthless in their onslaught against weeds. Church history furnishes many examples of attempts to root out error, heresy, and opposition. God's answer condones no complacent acceptance: "Let both grow together until the harvest." Violent weeding jeopardizes the wheat. Was Lincoln right in saying, "If you do the right thing in the wrong way, that's as bad as the wrong thing"? The day of separation comes. Life moves toward a climax. The Kingdom is crucial, and the final decision will be God's. Meanwhile, toil in patience and confidence that with God what should be shall be.

The Miracle of the Garden

The kingdom of God is as if a man should scatter seed upon the ground . . . and the seed should sprout and grow, he knows not how. . . . It is like a grain of mustard seed.

MARK 4:26-28, 30.

The miracle is the miracle of growth. Here is encouragement that all who work with plants, living or human, need. There is vitality in that tiny seed, in that little person. Teachers and parents may despair of their work. God has not forgotten. He cares for it, and the results will appear sooner than we think.

"We find great things are made of little things,
And little things go lessening till at last
Comes God behind them."

Illustrations from history, biography, and from your own observation will occur to you. You think of an old man remarking in the hearing of a little French girl, "God will one day raise up a deliverer for the French." How the seed thought grew! The little girl became Joan of Arc. That small boy, watching his father's agile fingers playing a harpsichord, wins from his father a word of encouragement: "Be patient, son, keep loving your music." That boy's name? Mozart. In a crowded English rectory a mother, hearing one of her many children pray, tells him she is sure that, if he is good, God will use him to help others. John Wesley. And Jesus! He "cast himself into the rough furrows of our little earth. The blade even now is visible. The harvest song shall one day be raised in joy."

A Gardener's Problem

A sower went out to sow.

MATTHEW 13:3.

Did you read that popular book last winter, or early spring, the seed catalogue? Because of previous disappointments, did you regard the descriptions and promises skeptically? Why are the results of our gardening often disheartening: seed, location of the garden, lack of green thumbs?

The Master Gardener faced a similar problem. His garden was the world, and his seed the truth of the gospel. Yet early he met striking differences in response. So he related his experience and explanation in the short story of the soils. We Christians cultivate our garden and face a similar problem. Why so little deep response to the truth? Why so many people untouched by the church and its message? Is it always the fault of the church, of the gardeners? It may be the fault of the soil. Many amateurs submit samples of their garden and lawn soil to a state agricultural station. Back come the analysis and recommendations as to what chemicals to add, and how much.

From some such introduction you proceed along the natural divisions of the parable.

I. *The beaten path.* The mind and spirit are hardened by ceaseless traffic of ideas and pressures. Prejudice and preoccupation harden the heart.

II. *Stony ground.* The shallow soul is like the shallow soil. Paul knew Athenians with such superficial minds. They were impulsive, quickly tired runners after each new thing. Consider the sporadic enthusiasms of nominal church members. Japanese gardeners stunt forest trees by tying up the taproot so that the young tree lives off surface roots. What was intended to become a forest giant ends up as a potted plant. Dwell deep.

III. *" Dirty " soil, dirty with weeds.* " The cares of the world " and the " delight in riches " crowd out the flowers and fruits of the Spirit. Artemus Ward once said of a man that " he tried to do too much and succeeded." When we are too busy to find time for the church, for its worship and friendships and service, we are too busy. Weed your garden, says the Master. " Create in me a clean heart, O God " (Ps. 51: 10).

IV. *But this soil analysis ends hopefully.* " Other seeds fell on good soil and brought forth grain." It produced a marvelous crop.

"The seed sown on good soil is the man who both hears and understands the message. His life shows a good crop" (Matt. 13:23, Phillips). Can soils be changed? A glorious fact of experience is that our lives can be. The hard life can be softened, the shallow life deepened, the crowded life be made simpler. For our Gardener is not only seedsman but plowman. Read John Masefield's "The Everlasting Mercy" again, particularly the lines:

> "O Christ who holds the open gate,
> O Christ who drives the furrow straight,
> O Christ, the plough . . .
> Lo, all my heart's field red and torn,
> And thou wilt bring the young green corn."

ASCENSION DAY

Sky Observers

Placards and newspaper announcements ask for civilians to serve as sky watchers. Civilian air defense authority is convinced that more of us need to watch the sky for strange aircraft and report them to air defense centers. Nineteen centuries ago there was a tiny group of sky watchers, "gazing into heaven" (Acts 1:10). They watched, not because of fear of an enemy who might swoop in upon them from the heavens, but because they were fascinated by the strange departure of their loved Leader. Their fear was the fear of abandonment by one whom they believed was Lord of heaven and earth, of time and eternity.

Men still watch the sky in fascination, in fear, and in horror. They watch rising, expanding clouds over Pacific islands and distant waters. Such observers justifiably experience awe and fear. To all of us the question asked of the disciples at the ascension of Christ is pertinent: "Why do you stand looking into heaven?" "Return to your Jerusalem," the Spirit of God seems to say. "Get on with your task of witnessing to the only power that can master the destructive force unleashed by modern atomic physicists. Repent and believe the gospel. Get into the upper room, as did the bewildered but trusting disciples."

Prayer and planning for common action is needed. Said the leading editorial in the *New York Herald Tribune* the day after an official confirmation of an atomic explosion was made, "We must be bigger men or be overwhelmed." Christians have the only ground for hope: God's loving, holy, and righteous purpose is declared in Jesus Christ. To link ourselves and other men of all nations with this purpose is now no longer a pious option. Now it can be — and not metaphorically — Christ or chaos.

You may find here in this thought of sky-watching an idea for another kind of sermon, one in which you will remind yourself and your people that even in a practical age and culture many still gaze into heaven, when the heaven in which they may live is as close as their need. Astrology, pagan "spiritism," and other superstitions of moderns represent sky-watching of the futile and even harmful kind. The answers they seek and the power they need for living comes from joining the redemptive and redeemed community of Christians, and finding in the fellowship of prayer and witness, of love and faith and hope, what none may find "gazing into heaven."

Visibility Zero

As they were looking on, he was lifted up, and a cloud took him out of their sight.

ACTS 1:9.

To have their risen Lord obscured by a cloud and to see him vanish shook the first disciples. If now he were forever remote from the world and from their struggles and needs, what was the good of all that he and they had endured? True, he might be in the heavens, at the center of universal power, but why could they not see him, feel him near? They could, and did! Clouds obscure the sun, and clouds in our skies obscure the Son — but he remains the light forever, ever shining.

Without the clouds, where would be faith? Without the clouds, how could we mature as adult members of God's family? Think of the "clouds" into which vanish persons and props on which we leaned too heavily. Also descending on many lives are the clouds of intellectual doubt, of moral perplexity, of spiritual uncertainty, of chilling and enveloping grief. But, as with Jesus on the mount of vision, there is a voice out of the cloud, our Companion on every road we take. "Visibility zero" may be the soul's weather report, but we learn — as John's Gospel declares — that it is a good thing for us that he should go away, that he may come again in the divine Helper, the Holy Spirit, the living Christ. (See John, ch. 16, as translated by J. B. Phillips in *The Gospels.*) For it remains true, far truer than the devout souls of the early church believed concerning a literal return "on the clouds," that "this Jesus, who was taken up from you into heaven, will come" through the clouds when we need him most. Meanwhile, "the climbing feet," the steadfast trust, the loyal service of Christ are essential even though he seems absent.

VI

WHITSUNTIDE

Season of the Holy Spirit
and of
the Birth and Expansion of the
Christian Church

WHITSUNDAY

(Pentecost)

Frustrated or Fruitful

Suppose the gospel ended where scholars think Mark's Gospel was abruptly broken off: "And they went out and fled from the tomb; for trembling and astonishment had come upon them; and they said nothing to any one, for they were afraid" (Mark 16: 8)? God's redemption in Christ's death and resurrection had taken place. His mighty acts had released mankind from the power of the enemy — evil, death, and all their vile allies. And yet the recipients of this glorious good news, the men and women who had experienced the power of his death and victory, "said nothing to anyone, for they were afraid of — " So James Moffatt translated the final verse of Mark. It would have been Christianity limited, faith frozen by fear, Christianity crippled and constricted. Suppose that the first Christians had stayed in that mood? The life-affirming, world-transforming enterprise might have been wholly other than it has been. Conceivably Christianity might have been one of many cults, or even a matter of antiquarian interest only. Of course, God being who he is, and having done what he has done, it is incredible that one group of disciples would have defeated his purpose.

But many Christians are living as if the resurrection and ascension ended the revelation and the revolution wrought by God. They say "nothing [at least not much that's convincing] to any one," for they are afraid. But we live after Pentecost, not before it. The acts of the apostles were set down, and the acts were the action of the Holy Spirit. It is a serial story, with no one knows how many installments yet to follow. One chapter may be written of our acts, if we strike to the deeper levels of the Christian experience.

In such a sermon you would "find" many good persons who are not unbelievers but who could honestly confess that the power and joy and certitude of the faith is rarely known by them. You would give a working description of the Holy Spirit—"God in action in human life."

Next you would answer the question, How and where do we receive Him who energizes and guides everyone who welcomes him? "They were all with one accord in one place" (Acts 2:1), and of "one accord" by reason of their common devotion to Christ. In this fact lies part of the answer as to where and how.

Next, to follow ancient and modern spiritual guides, we could indicate other steps in receiving the Spirit: (1) Believe that God intends you to receive him. (2) Be sure that you really want him in your life. (3) Pay the price, which is the surrender of yourself to him, without reservation and without agitation. (4) Take the gift so freely given. "You shall receive the gift of the Holy Spirit" (Acts 2:38). "How much more shall your heavenly Father give the Holy Spirit to them that ask him" (Luke 11:13). Take it; rather, take him, not dictating the terms or the manner of his coming. (5) Then live the life in the Spirit—the life of faith, of uncalculating service to Christ and others, the life of worship, witness, work—and joy and peace. A proof of the indwelling spirit is that we are fruitful, producing those fruits of the Spirit of which Paul wrote.

The Holy Spirit

A sermon on the Holy Spirit might instruct those who are spiritually members of the group Paul found at Ephesus, who had "never even heard that there is a Holy Spirit." Attention could be directed to what the Bible says about the Holy Spirit. In the Old Testament the belief develops and is gradually transformed into the power of an all-holy God, creator and redeemer. You may cite Ps. 139. The developing insight may be traced in such passages as Ex. 36:1 f.; Judg. 13:25; 14:6; I Kings 3:28; Ps. 139:7; and Joel 2:28 f. In the New Testament, Jeremiah's promise that the day would come when God's children would do his will freely without the compulsion of external law or demand is fulfilled.

The first mark of the Holy Spirit is the liberation from bondage to legalism and to external requirements. The second is realization that the Spirit is the very presence and life of God, in which believers live, move, and have their being. He is the unfailing spring of the water of life. Have we understood that in the New Testament Christians do not pray for the coming of the Spirit? It is he who enables them to pray. They need not plead for his coming, for he is never absent, but they need only to recall the relationship they sustain to God by his grace, and receive and know and rejoice in his strength. Thirdly, in the New Testament the primary work of the Holy Spirit is to create and sustain a common life, the community (communion) of the Spirit, "God's cooperative society," the church. New Testament Greeks had a word for this: *koinōnia.* (See Acts 1:14; 2:1; 2:44; 4:32; I Cor. 12:11.)

Point four on the meaning and work of the Holy Spirit in the New Testament is that the Holy Spirit teaches us the inclusive character of Christ and his mission. Under the tutelage of the Spirit, the most exclusive of the apostles realized that Christ is the head, not of one nation only, but of all nations. His salvation is for all men everywhere. Not pedigree or privilege, but humanity is the condition he has established for his healing and renewal.

The final point, and one that underscores the conclusive difference between belief in the Holy Spirit before and after Christ's coming, is that since Pentecost he has been known to be the Spirit of Christ. Alec R. Vidler has said, "In the fellowship of communion of the Spirit, men are brought, not into tune with an impersonal infinite, but into a personal relationship with Christ their Head."

What Does the Holy Spirit Do Today?

(1) He brings God near, to change, and empower, and guide. (2) He interprets Christ (John 16:12 f.). (3) He harmonizes and unifies individuals and communities. (4) He disturbs men and institutions when either become settled or complacent. (5) The Holy Spirit humbles and fortifies mankind, and, as a contemporary thinker puts it, fortifies by humbling.

A Series on the Church

(1) Holy (Heb., ch. 9; I Peter 2:9). (2) Catholic (Gal. 3:28). (3) Apostolic (Eph. 2:19-22). In such a series you might celebrate the unity, spiritual and yet to be realized, using the other word from the ancient creed, "One." Ephesians 4:4-6 and John 17:23 would furnish Scriptural foundation and expository material.

Right Church but Wrong Pew

And a young man named Eutychus was sitting in the window. He sank into a deep sleep as Paul talked still longer; and being overcome by sleep, he fell down from the third story and was taken up dead.

ACTS 20:9.

Eutychus was literally caught napping. A case for the defense could be made. Paul preached an unconscionably long sermon. Perhaps this is why all pulpits have a clock near them. Again, the building was poorly ventilated. (Human beings are extremely sensitive to drafts, heat, cold, noises in church buildings.) And Eutychus may have been weary. Late hours may have accounted for his fatigue. But he was young. And he missed a marvelous opportunity by falling asleep — and nearly missed all future opportunities by falling while asleep. Saint Paul was making his last visit to Eutychus' home town of Troas. May the real reason for his perilous nap have been his lack of interest in what was going on? Because Jerusalem did not know and was not interested in the things which belonged to peace she lost her soul. This is a time for greatness. But only those who are awake, alert, responsive, know and use it. " Awake, O sleeper, . . . and Christ shall give you light " and glorious adventures.

" Awake, my soul, and with the sun
Thy daily stage of duty run;
Shake off dull sloth, and joyful rise."

How Can You Tell?

" He's a Christian and really works at it."
" How can you tell? "

How can we? Paul is dogmatic about the nature of a Christian's character. He leads " a life worthy of God, who calls you into his own kingdom and glory " (I Thess. 2: 12). God came uniquely in his Son, Jesus Christ, that we might know what godlike living is, and by his help move near to it.

I. *A Christian is one who is Christlike.* This sounds pious and easy; it is neither. We become like that with which we habitually live. " To me to live is Christ." To attain his kind of living requires superhuman resources. To lead " a life worthy of God " means what — in the family, in the job, in the community, in the church?

II. *A Christian is one who accepts the impossible task of continuing Christ's witness,* ministry, dying, and resurrection within the community of the Spirit. As God sent Jesus, so Jesus sends us to proclaim the truth, to heal men's minds and bodies, to liberate the captive souls, and to capture every lost province of God's Empire of love for him. (See John 17: 18.)

III. *A Christian is one who finds Christ's kind of personality not unattainable,* and the service of his cause thrilling and increasingly satisfying because he lives in companionship with God himself. A few simple words of personal testimony as to how this friendship becomes more vivid and constant would be helpful.

What Goes On Here?

Not even the habitual joker who cites laughable sermon topics should miss the relevance of a topic like that, particularly if it was placed immediately after "11 A.M." What goes on here when men and women and children assemble for worship? A suitable, if not startlingly novel, text would be the majestic call to worship, Ps. 95:6, "O come, let us worship and bow down, let us kneel before the Lord our Maker!" Worship is something we do together. Granted to a company of seekers is that which no one may find alone. What is it? What do we share when in sincerity and truth we worship the great God who draws near in Jesus Christ? Alliteration here is hard to avoid, and three C's offer as many divisions or heads: commemoration, covenant, communion.

I. *Commemoration.* It does commemorate the past: Do this in remembrance. Remember all the way the Lord thy God led thee. Recall his mighty acts and his great redemption. God has visited and redeemed his people. But worship is more, does more, than commemorating, essential as such recollection may be.

II. *Covenant.* It is a covenant, a New Testament. The agreement is entered into, and renewed. God in Christ is the "party of the first part." Quote Jeremiah's report: "I will make a new covenant with the house of Israel." We pay our vows unto the Lord. We renew our part in the contract.

III. *Communion.* Yet highest of all is the privilege of worship that we call communion. Here is the living fellowship. It is with men and women of kindred spirit. More, it is communion, intimate contact with the unseen and living Lord. Here we become one in him with " all the servants of our king, in earth and heaven. . . . One church, above, beneath."

How do we win such marvelous privileges? Said John Bishop, " All that is needed is that minister and people should come together expecting to receive, sure that something is going to happen, that they are going to meet with God, and that God is going to meet with them."

TRINITY SUNDAY

The Trinity

Sabellius described the doctrine of the Trinity as belief in one God, existent in and manifest under three modes or aspects of being, and that these three aspects were purely temporary. I have never read or heard any definition that is intellectually completely satisfying. No wonder early Christian teachers employed all sorts of analogy, from clover to triangle. Thank God, we may believe and pray to one God as Father, Son, and Holy Spirit without being able to understand or even frame the doctrine.

Yet, great as is the mystery of the God whom we know, and faltering as may be our speech when we try to clarify the faith, a sermon on the Trinity may actually prove more "down to earth," as well as "out of this world," than we suspect. Here is a sermon outline, borrowed from E. Stanley Jones, suggesting three facts about God: (1) God *for* us. (2) God *with* us. (3) God *in* us. God for us is God the Father; God with us is the Son of his love, Jesus Christ; God in us is the Holy Spirit. Three facts are signified: the divine intention; the divine invasion; the divine indwelling. Rich textual basis and background is in John 14: 15-17; 15: 26-27.

The famous nineteenth-century English divine James Martineau stated the doctrine of the Trinity in ways few Trinitarians would reject: The Father is God in himself; the Son is God manifested in the universe and in history, and brought to focus in the frame of redemption; while in the Holy Spirit is God in communion with man's inner spirit.

God in Three Persons

This outline was prepared by the late Donald M. Baillie, distinguished Scottish theologian and effective preacher, whose posthumous volume of sermons is entitled, *To Whom Shall We Go?* Dr. Baillie's text was Matt. 28:19: "In the name of the Father, and of the Son, and of the Holy Ghost." Here in this mysterious doctrine is the gospel summed up.

I. *One God.* This is part of the good news. "A famous divine of the Middle Ages said wittily that the devil was the first grammarian, when he taught men to give a plural to the word 'God.'" We cannot divide our allegiance between two or more idols. But even this tremendous ethical monotheism, as we learned to speak of it in our "erudite" seminary days, proved inadequate. Two new facts of history and experience have changed men's thought of the infinite and eternal one God. They are:

II. *The fact of Jesus Christ.* He brought God near in a new, intimate, transforming way. Firm believers in the unity of God found themselves thinking of Jesus whenever they thought of God, the Creator and Father. They knew that God was like Christ and that God was in Christ. He was not God, for he suffered pain and death. He was truly man. He was the incarnation of God. "So they came to speak of the Father and the Son; and even if they couldn't quite explain it or think it out, it was at the very heart of their faith."

III. *The fact of Pentecost.* After Jesus vanished from their sight, his first followers were convinced that somehow he was with them still. Far more real than ever before was the divine presence. This was unforgettably true in their secret meeting place in a large room that they used for prayer and fellowship in Jerusalem. They were persuaded that they had not lost, nor ever could lose, either God or Jesus. They experienced a kind of new tidal wave of power rushing into and through their lives. God our Father who came near to us in Jesus is with us now forevermore in the power of his Spirit. So we know what God is and what he did for our salvation and what God does still in us today. Thus, as Professor Baillie said, " the Church never tires of singing in gratitude: 'Glory be to the Father, and to the Son, and to the Holy Ghost; as it was in the beginning, is now, and ever shall be, world without end.' "

NATURE SUNDAY AND SUMMERTIME

Out of Doors with the Master

I. *Gardens.* "And the Lord God planted a garden eastward in Eden" (Gen. 2:8). "He went forth with his disciples over the brook Cedron, where was a garden. . . . Jesus ofttimes resorted thither with his disciples" (John 18:1-2). "Now in the place where he was crucified there was a garden; and in the garden a new sepulchre" (John 19:41).

Few are immune to the appeal of a garden. Tenement dwellers keep window boxes. Why is it so? Man's organic relationship to the soil? A race memory from the days when man earned his bread by growing it? Perhaps Genesis is nearer the truth: "God planted a garden." Human life had this for its early environment. God's Son loved a garden. But the first garden of the Bible was not the setting of a perfect idyll. You can be nearer the heart of evil than of God in a garden. Beauty is truth; so also is cruelty, selfishness, and sin. "In the place where he was crucified there was a garden." But John saw through that garden and saw that the jagged tree of the cross blossoms with love and faith. In the place where the Lord of life triumphed over sin and death there was a garden. For the eyes of faith every flower speaks of resurrection.

II. *Hills.* "I will lift up mine eyes unto the hills" (Ps. 121:1). Have we sufficiently considered the influences of hills and mountains on people and on human history? They have acted as barriers, obstacles, lines of defense, and sources of independence.

Then reflect on the hills in Jesus' life: Mt. Hermon, Calvary, and the others. What are the hills for? (1) For vision. (2) For climbing. (3) For communion. Yet actual summits do not bring us nearer to God than does a valley.

> " But God was not on the high hill,
> On the high hill apart,
> God was not on the high hill,
> Not being in my heart."

Another approach would be to start with John Henry Jowett's declaration that every person needs to have certain hills in his landscape. What hills? Sinai (law), Calvary (love), Olivet (life eternal).

III. *Roads.* " A highway shall be there " (Isa. 35:8). " By faith Abraham obeyed when he was called to go out to a place which he was to receive as an inheritance; and he went out " (Heb. 11:8). " Jesus said. . . , I am the way " (John 14:6).

To Isaiah, the highway home will be God's gift to weary exiles. (A sermon almost preaches itself from the passage beginning with verse eight in Isa., ch. 35.) What of the lure of the more or less open road today? Symbolism of the road continues to appeal to thoughtful pilgrims. Hilaire Belloc was sure that the road is one of the great fundamental institutions of mankind: determiner of city sites, controller of battle strategies, framer of economic development, channel of trade, artery of ideas.

But the real romance of roads is written in the Bible. Highways, journeys, wayfarers, obstacles, the Guide, and journey's end are described. Then reflect on the roads traveled to God, and the road down which God comes to his wandering children. God is the road maker, and he himself in the person of his Son is our Guide deep into his heart: " I am the way." Christ blazes the trail. He is the Guide, furnishing direction and companionship, a goal and power to reach it. " This is the way, walk in it " (Isa. 30:21). And the road leads home — not back, but forward to our true home. Who would not " labor night and day, to be a pilgrim "?

IV. *Trees.*

> " This is the Eternal's word:
> . . . Happy he who relies on the Eternal,
> with the Eternal for his confidence!
> He is like a tree planted beside a stream,
> reaching its roots to the water;
> untouched by any fear of scorching heat,
> its leaves are ever green,
> it goes on bearing fruit in days of drought,
> and lives serene."
>
> — *Jeremiah 17: 5-8* (*Moffatt*)

Most of us respond to the beauty of trees, except when autumn brings leaf-raking chores. Trees are more than scenic: they are essential to human life. Erosion, which spells disaster, follows destruction of forests. Yet it is not for utility but for beauty and healing that we chiefly cherish trees. " The groves were man's first temples." But nature cannot heal our deepest wounds. A vague pantheism is impotent to transform personal tragedy into peace and triumph. Equipped with Christian faith, we hear trees speak to us of the beauty and wisdom of God.

Jeremiah's little poem helps us to read God's alphabet in green. What do we read? (1) Rootage is important. (2) Reliance on God provides never-failing springs of vitality. " Remember Jesus . . . crucified [upon a tree] and risen." "Into the woods my Master went . . . Out of the woods He came." (3) There is a tree whose leaves are for the healing of souls and of nations. It is the tree of life because from it reigns the life-giver, Christ the Lord.

Other sermons of this general nature may be inspired by leaves (see Gen. 1: 11; Ps. 72: 6); stars (Ps. 147: 4; Rev. 2: 28; 22: 16); rainbows (Gen. 9: 13; Rev. 4: 3). For a sermon on the question " Who Owns the Garden? " see the parable in Luke 20: 9-18, noting v. 13: " Then the owner of the vineyard said, ' What shall I do? I will send my beloved son; it may be they will respect him.' " If service is the rent we pay for our room on earth, to whom do we pay it? If all derives from God, is ultimately his, then life is an entrustment. But life is also a glorious privilege. We toil not only under the great Taskmaster's eye; we join him as, in a profound sense, junior partners in his tremendous enterprise.

From communing with nature's God, our Creator, we commune with him who brings the Creator near as Redeemer. Indeed, only as we maintain this holy communion can we touch the glory of his robe in the world which he makes more than passing fair. Here is a theme you may find appealing as you prepare for a service in which Holy Communion is both description and goal.

"Knee-deep in June"

The world of nature is God's world, and nature itself the garment of the Creator-Spirit. Preachers have the highest authority, not to indulge in sentimental homilies on birds, bees, and flowers, but to use God's nonhuman activity and creatures as a kind of schoolmaster to lead men to Christ.

Our Lord loved hills that ran up into the sky. Lake and river, grass and flowers, clouds and birds and trees must have been studied lovingly by the divine artist, for his recorded sayings carry so many references to them. Not only the market place, but the good earth which knew seedtime and harvest furnished him with unforgettable parables and word pictures. Why not emulate him in this also? Even second-generation city dwellers are not so far from the farm. What urban executive does not dream of "a place in the country"? You may wish it otherwise when a certain lady reminds you of grass to be cut or a flower garden to be weeded, but we humans sustain an organic relationship to the soil.

A suitable text would be Matt. 24:32-33: "From the fig tree learn its lesson: as soon as its branch becomes tender and puts forth its leaves, you know that summer is near. So also, when you see all these things, you know that he is near, at the very gates." In our hemisphere June corresponds to that time in the East when the fig tree bursts out in full leaf. From there you follow the thought that One draws near to us, in the promise of the seasons, in the tragic and hopeful events of our time, in the mercy and judgment of God in Christ. If only we could and would see! Grim as is the prospect confronting the nations in this time of trouble, our hope is in God. Sang G. A. Studdert-Kennedy, who was no Pollyanna:

> "There is love behind the splendour
> Of the spring,
> When the weary winter dies
> And the Lord with laughing eyes
> Bids the trembling world arise,
> Whispering,
> 'Did ye think that God was dead?
> Nay, my blood is warm and red,
> And there is no death to dread —
> Come and sing.'"

Then this poet-preacher made the response our preaching should evoke:

> "Lord, I pray thee give my spirit
> Eyes to see,
> Through the things of time and space,
> All the glories of thy grace,
> The commandment of thy face
> Bidding me
> Follow on where thou hast trod
> Though I share the grief of God.
> Give me strength to sweat my blood,
> Lord, for thee."
> — *Geoffrey A. Studdert-Kennedy*

"Worship That Makes the Heart Glad"

Here is a sermon to teach our wandering folk that wherever they wander, in summer or in any season, worship is essential and lifts the most jaded heart. The text is from Ps. 122. "This," says our expositor, "is worship that makes the heart glad."

I. *True worship of God saves us from the evils of idolatry.* If we will not worship the God of revelation, we will worship something or someone: abstract ideas, personal ambition, mammon, or even our own image.

II. *True worship of God unites us in ever larger unities.* Vital religion draws together men and women of diverse backgrounds of race, origin, political opinion, and social class on the deepest level — spiritual fellowship.

III. *True worship "lifts men's minds above themselves and increases the joy of God-centeredness."* When prayer and praise in social worship are neglected, is it not true that psychological clinics are overcrowded? Sanity, peace, and joy come when we lose ourselves in adoration of the great God who made and saved us. "Come let us join our cheerful songs, with angels round the throne."

Mountains of the Bible

A series on mountains of the Bible and of Christian experience may appeal to you: (1) The mount of trial (Matt. 4:8). (2) The mount of choice (Mark 3:13). (3) The mount of service (Matt. 15:29-31). (4) The mount of agony (Matt. 26:30). (5) The mount of glory (Matt. 27:33). (6) The mount of final command (Matt. 28:16).

A Summer Series

Capturing interest in the long summer season is a series based on Ps. 121: (1) God of the waiting hills. (2) God of the sleepless watch. (3) God of the friendly shade. (4) God of the windy road.

"The Noise of Archers"

August dog days find most preachers responsive to any apology for idleness. One active Christian worker, when recently asked what he intended to do on his vacation, quickly and understandably answered, " Just sleep! " God ordered life on the basis of what pundits call the principle of alternation: toil and rest, work and leisure.

In a world like this, and in seasons like summer in our Western Hemisphere, we need to be " delivered from the noise of archers in the places of drawing water." This is the quaint translation of the King James Version of Judg. 5: 11. (It might provide a text and setting for a sermon on " Take It Easy.") Today's equivalent of " the noise of archers " would include the hum of factory machines, the buzzing of telephones, the clatter of organization wheels, and the dull rumble of routine. Our Lord urged his first followers, " Come away by yourselves to a lonely place, and rest a while " (Mark 6: 31). Isolation, rest, and true relaxation have therapeutic value for the soul as for the body. An old spiritual directs us to " stand right still and steady " ourselves.

Busyness, even in our Lord's service, may have a more deadly result than jangled nerves, frayed tempers, and poisonous fatigue. The Church of Saint Peter can become the Church of Saint Vitus. For the communion of saints we can substitute the commotion of the saints. Instead of going about doing good we may settle for just going about. Agitation and activity, even on behalf of a program, may find us hustling on the periphery instead of digging at the center of the faith.

Consider I Kings 20: 40. In this chapter we have one of the acted parables that delighted Old Testament prophets. Details are not significant. What is worth noting and thinking about is the insistence upon doing the task committed to us by God, and the tragedy of missing it by being busy about other things. This is the point of the sentence, " And as your servant was busy here and there, he was gone."

More than one perceptive Christian has seen those words as the possible epitaph of a church, even of a prosperous, crowded, and highly organized church. Conscientious ministers and laymen can be so busy keeping the organization's machinery operating smoothly, being all things to all people, " implementing " the principles and ideals, that He is gone whom they seek to serve and introduce to persons who know him not. It is hard for us activists to realize that Christianity, as demonstrated in the New Testament, is not primarily activity, essential as activity may be. It is an attitude, a relationship, a commitment to God as he reveals himself and meets us in Jesus Christ.

So in the August days, when there is less that is audible and visible going on in most churches, we might hold a few quiet conversations with our gracious Lord. In his presence you and I might raise some relevant questions. What is the one supreme thing in our discipleship? What is the top priority among the objectives? Spreading wholesome ideals or opening the way for the Holy Spirit to make Christian men and Christian women? Formulating sensible views on politics, war, communism, or anything else—or attaining the mind of Christ on such issues?

"Loaf and invite the soul," exhorted Walt Whitman. The counsel is sound. But let's use these fleeting summer days to invite the soul to face the autumn and winter schedule in the light of Christ. In Christ's company we can rearrange those priorities. We can even discover certain emphases we ought to make in the year ahead. If we do, it is unlikely that, when we resume full activity in September, we shall miss the point or him.

VII

KINGDOMTIDE

Season of the Kingdom of God on Earth

FESTIVAL OF CHRIST THE KING

Who's Winning?

You asked the question when you came late to the game, either when you watched it " live " on the field or on the TV screen. Sometimes the neighbors ask it when they hear Junior and Dad arguing over the use of the car. Concerning deeper, more baffling conflicts men are asking the same question. Who's winning, Russian communism or Western democracy? peace or war? In the light of atomic warfare, will it be life or death? Christ or Antichrist?

Luke reports the verdict of the Lord of history. During his earthly life Jesus had commissioned seventy — or seventy-two — of his men and women to engage in a mission to those living in territory occupied by the enemy. It was not a preparatory mission. His instructions indicate that the disciples were to proclaim everywhere the astonishing news that in Christ the Kingdom of God had come near. It was here, and it was available. His representatives would be the agents and instruments of this Kingdom and of the King himself.

When they returned, mission accomplished, they told him excitedly of their extraordinary success. Even the demonic forces in the situation yielded to his power, mediated through them. Then Jesus almost ecstatically told them of the true meaning of their achievement: " And he said to them, ' I saw Satan fall like lightning from heaven ' " (Luke 10: 18). In their witness and in their service he saw the powers of darkness dethroned, beaten, and ultimately destroyed. He knew the score.

Would he say that today? If he did — and he does through the Holy Spirit speaking in his church — how many would agree? Here you could deal with the other verdicts.

I. *Secular despair*. Thoughtful, informed men who do not share the faith of Christ are convinced that the foreseeable future is dark. Some feel that illimitable power is now at the disposal of irresponsible, cruel men. The A-, the H-, the cobalt bombs are here. In the places of decision are persons determined to dominate the rest of mankind. The " little people " who could influence many of the " mighty " are complacent, or hysterical, or " they couldn't care less." There are more hopeless people in the world today than people with false hopes.

II. *Secular and religious optimism*. This mood may not be widespread, but it is held. Science, education, the inventiveness of man, and the steady gains of " civilization " seem to these optimists far greater than the dark facts. Religious optimists point to the immense and heartening growth of churches, at least in North America. They remind us that on the clock of time it is only a few minutes since Christianity began its world-encircling movement.

III. *Christian realism*. This is the attitude that tries to see the picture " steadily and to see it whole." It is believing realism. Acknowledged is the stubborn evil in us all. So also is God in Christ. History may be " open at both ends," with continuing possibilities of good and evil. But the final score is certain: " He shall reign." " The kingdoms of this world " shall become " the kingdom of our Lord, and of his Christ " — if not in what we call history, then beyond it. Remember the story alleged to have happened during one of the fierce persecutions in the early years of the faith? A pagan friend of a Christian stood beside him as both watched numbers of the faithful thrown into the arena to be tortured and slain. He asked the Galilean's follower: " Where is your Carpenter now? " Replied the Christian, " Making a coffin for your emperor." Do we believe it? Only those "in Christ" have such assurance.

IV. *What must we do in the light of this conviction?* (1) "Every one who thus hopes in him purifies himself"—not merely by denying himself sensual indulgence, or the cheap luxury of pious resignation to grim conditions and tendencies in our society. We equip ourselves to engage in an "engagement very difficult," as Cromwellian patriots expressed it. We go "active" out of the "reserve" Christian army. (2) We conduct ourselves with what has been called "true Christian nonchalance." This means yielding neither to complacency nor to panic. We are those who live between D-Day and V-Day. Therefore, we shall fear, not those who may destroy the body, but only those who can harm the soul. By our faithful witness where we live and in our daily job, and by our unfaltering loyalty to our divine Commander and to his church, we shall move forward with him, knowing that victory has been won in advance. One day we may hear him say, "As you toiled and witnessed and lived the life for me down there in Podunk—or wherever it was that we lived—'I saw Satan fall like lightning from heaven.'"

What's Your Picture of God?

Gilbert K. Chesterton was sure that a landlady's view of the universe, of the nature of ultimate reality, was more important to know than the rates she charged and the kind of lodging-house she kept. How do we think of God? An overwhelming majority of North Americans avow belief in God. What kind of God? A blind, cosmic urge? A principle of concentration? A super Santa Claus? An arbitrary dictator? Relentless law? Unknowable? The omnicompetent state? "To us," affirms Paul on behalf of all Christians, "there is but one God, the Father, of whom are all things, and we in him; and one Lord Jesus Christ, by whom are all things, and we by him" (I Cor. 8:6). What is the character of this Christian God, this God who confronts us in nature, in history, in man, and supremely and redemptively in the total fact of our Lord Jesus Christ? Why not give Jesus' account of the character of God?

I. *To our Lord, God is the " Father in heaven,"* who is " good " with a goodness beyond justice (Mark 10: 18; Matt. 5: 45; Luke 6: 35; Matt. 20: 1-15).

II. *He persistently takes the initiative* in providing good gifts for his creatures (Matt. 6: 33-34).

III. *He is goodness supported by adequate power* (Mark 10: 27; 14: 36). As the eminent Biblical scholar and theologian Dr. C. H. Dodd states in *The Bible Today,* " This account he made credible through the effect of what he was and what he did." This great and gracious God confronts us in Christ, in the energy of holy and righteous love " that makes a decisive impact upon those who come within his orbit," transforming events and situations, because it is the power of the living God.

Are You Looking in the Wrong Place?

Why do you seek the living among the dead?

LUKE 24: 5.

This is the question for the person who rejects Christianity as " the great illusion." It is also addressed to the reluctant skeptic who would believe but cannot, because he feels that the evidence is insufficient. Many nominal Christians who sigh, " Where is the blessedness I knew when first I saw the Lord? " should stop sighing and start looking in the right place.

One future minister of the Presbyterian Church in England, submitting an outline on this text at Westminster College, Cambridge, offered useful directions: Look for the living Lord, not in argument about him, not in dogma, not in nature, of which admittedly he is Lord, nor even in history. Christ is more than a fact "stranded amid the years." Look for him in (1) the Scriptures of our Testaments, which testify to him; (2) in that mysterious and real encounter called prayer; and (3) in the encounter that comes when we draw near in faith as he draws near in his truth and goodness and mystery.

The Key to Life's Mystery

For now we see in a mirror dimly, but then face to face.
I CORINTHIANS 13: 12.

At present all we see is the baffling reflection of reality; we are like men looking at a landscape in a small mirror. The time will come when we shall see reality whole and face to face! At present all I know is a little fraction of the truth, but the time will come when I shall know it as fully as God now knows me! (PHILLIPS.)

I. *We live in a mysterious universe.* The more we know, the deeper grows the mystery. This fact is ignored, or not known, by many who feel that science banishes all mystery. But ask the scientists! How much simpler and clearer life and the universe seemed to our ancient forefathers who lived in a tidy little system, on a world which was flat, central, dominating! Consider also the mystery of personality, the strange complex of genes, glands, instinctive drives, Godward and demonic impulses. Reflect on the mysterious " subbasement " of the unconscious or subconscious and of the deep racial memory which sometimes surges to the surface.

II. *The Bible and Christ himself deepen the mystery.* Certainly the Bible, far from clarifying all that baffles, acknowledges the clouds and darkness around God, and over life. Quote such passages from Paul's writings as Rom. 11: 33-35. Recall Jesus' acknowledgment that some things were known only to the Father and that his disciples could not receive them at their human stage of development. Does not the cross itself deepen the mystery for the Christian believer? Who was it that asked, " My God, why? "

III. *Christ is the key to the mystery.* He is the revelation of the innermost reality. In his life, death, and resurrection, and in his

Spirit and teachings, we find the master clue to the understanding of the mystery. We have not all the answers, but we have Christ, who is the answer. We have not all the light that we might desire. But God, in giving us Christ, who is the Light of the World, has given us, as Robert Browning said, "light enough in the dark to rise by, and we rise." Does it not strengthen baffled, perplexed pilgrims to know that Christ is the way, the truth, and the light as well as the life? At the heart of existence is a loving purpose and a Companion for every dark valley.

God's Gift of Turbulence

Like an eagle that stirs up its nest, that flutters over its young, spreading out its wings, catching them, bearing them on its pinions, the Lord alone did lead [Jacob, who here personified the nation].

DEUTERONOMY 32: 11-12.

One of God's choicest gifts is peace, between nations or in the individual soul. General Sherman's well-known definition of war is true. Christ's sovereign cure for conflict, tension, and turmoil remains unchallenged. "Peace at the center" is one of his incalculably precious boons. But this is only one half of the truth. He also brings challenge, conflict, and war. Cite New Testament sayings of our Lord that stress this.

Sometimes on commercial plane flights the pilot's voice, heard over the public address system, says: "We are approaching an area of turbulence. Please fasten your seat belts." If anyone goes with Christ, he may be sure that such companionship will bring him into areas of conflict, turbulence, and storm. "If you have not got a cross," said the Scottish reformer, Samuel Rutherford, "you have not got Christ, for it is one of the first of his gifts." Psalm 112:7 makes clear that such turbulence is not withheld from God's chosen: "It is the wicked who saith in his heart, I shall not be moved: for I shall never be in adversity."

If God is all that Christ claimed and unveiled, why does God permit such turbulence? A clue to the answer is found in the famous "Song of Moses." Whether actually written by Moses or not, it reflects his world-view, his theology, and his working philosophy. The writer recounts God's providential acts on behalf of Israel. God chose this people, saved them, loved and led them. The people were often perverse and rebellious. Just when they seemed safest and most secure, he let them be uprooted. "As an eagle stirreth up her nest . . . so the Lord . . ." Picture the young birds' first response: "What's come over mother? You call this love? Pushing us out into the wild blue yonder?" But the seeming cruelty was true love, and the only way to maturity.

I. *God shakes the foundations of the common life* that men and women may realize that God alone is supreme and that his righteousness is the only foundation that endures. See Heb. 12:26-28 — in particular v. 28, with its gratitude for "receiving a kingdom that cannot be shaken."

II. *God stirs up the church* by population changes and social crises of one kind or another, that his people may find new opportunities of witnessing and serving. Dr. John Heuss has some scorching and relevant words for the church that hugs to its frigid bosom the outworn concepts and programs of a defunct Victorianism. It's not "peace, perfect peace" that many congregations should either pray for or sing about, but, "Awake, our souls, stretch every nerve." The Anglican prayerbook collect for the Sunday before Advent is appropriate: "Stir up, we beseech thee, O Lord, the wills of thy faithful people."

III. *God thrusts us out of our snug nests* that we may learn how to "mount up with wings like eagles, . . . run and not be weary, . . . walk and not faint." Illustrations from biography, or from your own experience of what seemed a catastrophe and proved to be a means of grace, will help. Albert Edward Day, in *Autobiography of Prayer,* tells of his own crisis caused by incipient tuberculosis, and of God's marvelous answer to his poignant prayer for help. "Because they have no changes, . . . they fear not God," say the Scriptures. Christ who said, "My peace I give to you," also said, "I have not come to bring peace, but a sword."

LABOR SUNDAY

The Christian as Servant

September opens with that slightly misnamed holiday, Labor Day. You may have thoughtfully arranged to conclude your vacation after that weekend, when few labor except the parson. But September marks resumption of toil in most churches, even though, in our increasingly telescoped church year, October's first Sunday celebrates the rallying of our forces. As a trumpeter of the Lord, you will be sounding the reveille, the call to rise and serve. Every year we confront stragglers, the complacent, the unresponsive. Why not make an indirect attack on these by reminding them that the Christian is a servant, who works no union hours, and who must labor, as Loyola's prayer puts it, without any thought of reward save that he does the Master's will. Scripture relevant to such a message will be found in Mark 10: 42-45; II Cor. 4: 5; and I Cor. 9: 19-22.

The 1950 U. S. census showed 25 per cent fewer domestic servants than in 1940. Despite inconvenience to harassed homemakers, this gradual disappearance of household employees is salutary. Christianity has contributed to the gradual abolition of the master-servant relationship. The magazine *Fortune,* in a recent article on the " servant problem," concluded that " Americans don't like to be servants."

Human beings don't like to be servants. " Servant " connotes servitude. Christ came to make men free. True, Saint Paul's admonitions to Christian slaves seem a negation of Christ's law. For an illustration, see Dr. Howard Thurman's little book *Jesus and the Disinherited,* and the autobiographical recollection of his grandmother's refusal to have any of Paul's writings read to her. We must acknowledge that the great apostle may have had a blind spot, due largely to the situation in which he found himself. Moreover, Paul was a privileged person, and no one could treat him as a slave.

But Jesus was denied full citizenship in his nation. He knew the plight of servants. Yet this Man insists that his followers must be slaves of others for the Kingdom's sake. Let the preacher admit that he doesn't enjoy the status of servant. Who wants to be at everyone's beck and call? Who wants to be pushed around, imposed upon, his rights and privileges trampled underfoot? Yet Christ declares that greatness in his society depends, not on being "top dog," but on being a servant of all. To choose a Christian vocation is to choose the role of servant. Every Christian is a minister, a servant. We cannot soften his demand. Perhaps one of the better popes was on the main line when he chose as a title, "Servant of the servants of God."

Christ who makes the demand supplies the grace to fulfill it. Keep close to him and in the company of his faithful servants.

"One Kingdom only is divine,
One banner triumphs still;
Its King a servant, and its sign
A gibbet on a hill."
— *Godfrey Fox Bradby*

We had better get used to being servants. If we are with Christ and "in Christ," we shall be serving a long, long time. In heaven, says the author of The Revelation (ch. 7:15), "they . . . serve him day and night within his temple."

Kenneth J. Foreman relates a whimsical dream. At the admissions office in heaven, a bustling tycoon brushed past the waiting line of applicants. Saint Peter smiled, asked him what he would like to be now that he was in the celestial realm. The self-important executive gulped. He offered a pious answer in the words of the only hymn he could recall: "I want to be an angel and with the angels stand." The "big fisherman" smiled disarmingly. In the manner of an expert personnel man, he asked, "What experience have you had?"

Carpet Sweepers and Crowns

At the time of the coronation of Queen Elizabeth II, unrepentant republicans were thrilled by the radio, TV, and movie portrayals of the gorgeous pageantry and moving religious symbolism of that service. Did you read of the story of the four charwomen? At the final rehearsal a little episode occurred in a moment of great tension. The orchestra's final strains sounded, the archbishop stood by the altar, and nearby were grouped officers of the state. Then came the spine-tingling fanfare of trumpets. The queen was about to enter. "Suddenly," wrote Beverley Nichols, a British author who was present, "onto this scene of awe and splendor trotted four charwomen. Four ladies in white overalls, brandishing, not swords, or plumes, or gaiters, or any emblem of state, but four carpet sweepers. Completely undeterred, and with typical British phlegm, they proceeded to trot around the very throne itself, energetically pursuing pieces of fluff and feather which had drifted onto the golden carpet. And equally suddenly the vast assembly, for all its loyalty and all its awe, realized that this was in fact an enchantingly humorous situation, and laughed loud, and long, to the very roof." Incidentally, can you imagine that sound in any assembly met to honor a Hitler or a Stalin? In the actual service, any laughter was lost in the stupendous burst of organ music the Earl Marshal arranged to cover up the entrance of the four charwomen.

Carpet sweepers in a coronation! Life's sublime moments show the significance of homely, humdrum service. A person's task may seem trivial. His fidelity, his thoroughness, his dependability are never trivial. If the four charwomen had merely gone through the motions, a hitch in the solemn proceedings might have occurred. A prelate or a princeling, even the queen, might have sneezed! More serious consequences may ensue when our humble task is treated carelessly. "Remember," said a sign in an aircraft factory during wartime, "a concealed mistake may cost a brave man his life."

Could you not take the theme from there, and perhaps emphasize the Christian perspective? "I am among you as one who serves," said the King of Glory (Luke 22:27). He is faithful in small things (Luke 16:10). Look at John, ch. 13, where he who might have taken a star took a towel and a basin. What if he has chosen us, and ordained us, to push a carpet sweeper, a pen, a typewriter; buy and sell necessities; teach youngsters the way to live as God's children within his family? Are we not then in "holy orders" in a Christian vocation?

"Work is devout, and service is divine.
Who stoops to scrub a floor
May worship more
Than he who kneels before a holy shrine."

In a socially useful occupation the motive, the dedication, is everything. George Herbert knew:

"Teach me, my God and King,
In all things thee to see;
And what I do in anything,
To do it as for thee."

Are we not commissioned to help those who see nothing divine in their drudgery to attain the mind of Christ? Carpet sweepers and their American equivalent can prepare the way for the coming of the King of Kings. Does he not come through the faithful, honest, second-mile service of "little people"? Have you come across this infrequently read bit of Scripture: "These were the potters, and those that dwelt among plants and hedges; there they dwelt with the king for his work" (I Chron. 4:23).

Don't Relax

Here is a counsel flagrantly contradictory to much current religious or pseudo-religious advice. So be it. The art of relaxation is one that all need to cultivate — some of the time. More imperative for Christian action is the ability to be properly worked up concerning vital issues. Winston Churchill, in a moving "sermon" to the House of Commons and to the world on March 2, 1955, said: "What ought we to do? Which way shall we turn to save our lives and the future of the world? . . . What would lie before them [the children] if God wearied of mankind?" Churchill was properly tense. Here, then, is a text for a meditation for good people who think chiefly of relaxation, which, of course, the Lord wants them to enjoy, provided it is for recharging their spiritual batteries and strengthening their moral muscles for the burdens he wants them to carry.

See Gal. 6: 6-10, noting particularly v. 9: "And let us not grow weary in well-doing," which may be freely translated to read: "Don't get tired of doing the fine thing, for, when the proper time comes, we shall reap so long as we don't relax our efforts. So, then, as we have opportunity, let us do good to all, especially to those who are members of the household of the faith."

Underscore those words of the intensely practical Paul, "So long as we don't relax our efforts." It's a rather grim text for easy-going moderns, but there it is in vs. 7-8. If a man allows the "soft" side of his nature to dominate, he can expect only a harvest of trouble.

A wise Biblical teacher of Glasgow, Prof. William Barclay, wrote: "If a man keeps on always walking the high way, and always doing the fine thing, he may have to wait long, but in the end God repays. Christianity never took the threat out of life." But Paul finishes by reminding his companions that while sometimes the duty and work of Christian generosity and service may be irksome, the duty remains. "Don't relax" in the service of Christ! "Let us not grow tired of doing good," is J. B. Phillips' paraphrase of the verse, "for, unless we throw in our hand, the ultimate harvest is assured."

WORLD-WIDE COMMUNION

A New Fellowship

A rich mine awaits exploration in Ex. 24:9-11: "Then Moses and Aaron, Nadab, and Abihu, and seventy of the elders of Israel went up, and they saw the God of Israel. . . . And he did not lay his hand on the chief men of the people of Israel; they beheld God, and ate and drank."

What they saw in God created a new fellowship with one another, and their meal was a symbol of unity, of the signing of a covenant, or the ratification of a pact.

Why Does Christ Come?

If we observe the wise rule of the Reformers, we shall have the Word both read and preached when we have a service of Holy Communion. At such a time, however, the Word preached will be of a devotional character and the sermon or meditation very much shorter than at other services. Since one of the most familiar, as well as one of the most significant, names for this central service of the Church is Communion, we do well to remind ourselves and our fellow communicants that this implies belief in the "real presence" of the risen Lord. Of course, we cannot limit him to one method of manifestation; he makes himself known to whom and where he chooses. Who would deny the experience of his presence to Quakers, who do not celebrate the sacrament outwardly? Yet the church witnesses to the fact that in the supreme act of our worship Christ comes in a special way. Argument as to the mode of his coming is usually fruitless, and certainly inappropriate when we gather about the Lord's Table.

Here is a theme for a Communion meditation suggested by Dr. Olive Wyon:

"With desire I have desired to eat this passover with you" (Luke 22:15). Jesus' ardent wish finds vivid expression in J. B. Phillips' version: "You do not know how I have longed to eat this Passover with you."

Your introduction could declare the church's claim that the real presence is manifested in the total action of Communion. You could then suggest that we come primarily to obey his command. Therefore our question should be, not, Why should I go? but, instead, Why does Christ come to us in this way?

Here are the four answers: (1) He comes because he desires us. This is the reason stated in his words to the first disciples: "I am here for you, because I want you for myself." He loves us, and to love is to want to be with the beloved. (2) He wants to lead us into his friendship. He comes not only as the King of heaven, but as our Friend. Does not the new covenant in his blood speak louder than any word? (3) He comes to make us strong. Not just to feel strong, but to be strengthened with might by his spirit within us — "strong to work, to endure, to love, and hope, and pray, and give." (4) He comes to transform us. At tremendous cost he gives himself to us that we may become more like him. So we pray: "Here, O Lord, we present ourselves. . . . Do with us and in us and through us according to thy will."

Once at a simple and unforgettable Communion service at a historic little church on the banks of the Red River in Manitoba, the late Dr. Charles W. Gordon exclaimed as he stood at the Lord's Table, "The Lord is as real to me as he was to Peter, or James, or John!" Looking at his radiant face and recalling his own exploits for Christ's cause, we students knew that his testimony was true. So may all God's people know the mystery of his presence in the "mystery of consecration" to Christ.

On Cultivating a Good Memory

Do you not remember?

MARK 8:18.

Anyone can have a good memory. This is the claim of Christianity. A good memory is one that recollects whatsoever things are true, honorable, just, pure, lovely, and gracious. Salvation is memory at its dynamic best. Memory may be a powerful agent of God in developing a more Christlike personality and a more Christian community. To a surprising degree, Jesus relied on the power of memory to save and keep men and women. Mark 8:10-21 provides an illustration.

But a good memory in a Christian sense is not simply a kind of Univac machine which produces memories that are delightful because only happy experiences or thoughts are inserted. How different history might be if men and leaders of men had remembered what led to earlier tragedies and disasters. Yet some persons are miserable because they do not put from them the memory of "old, unhappy, far-off things"—sins, humiliations, injuries—and battles of long ago. Like God, we must learn to cast our forgiven sins behind our backs and "remember them no more."

I. *Increasing faith.* A good Christian memory will increase faith and hold us steadfast in discouraging hours. Luke 24:2, 8, in J. B. Phillips' translation, reads: "Remember [what] He said to you, while He was still in Galilee. . . . Then they did remember what He said, and they turned their backs on the tomb." Remembering what God said and did in Christ can help us to turn our backs on the tombs of yesterdays' despairs and fears. "Remember all the way which the Lord your God has led you" and take courage, being "steady as you go."

II. *Recovering self-respect.* Another high use of Christian memory is to recover self-respect. "Who speaks for man?" asked Norman Cousins a short time ago. Not many, unless they hold the Christian doctrine of man. "We are God's children now." Remember! We have been loved, died for.

III. *Building hope.* Christian memory, which recalls and lives in the acts of God in Christ, is an angel of hope for tomorrow. "Remember, Jesus Christ . . . crucified . . . risen." So long his power has blest us, sure it still will lead us on, "o'er moor and fen, o'er crag and torrent, till the night is gone." Christ instituted the simplest meal imaginable so that we should have divine aid to memory. And remembering his sacrifice and continuing love and victory as we partake of this sacrament, we not only remember but have communion. "Do you not remember?"

Our Lord's Other Prayer

An expository study of John, ch. 17, may meet a continuing need. Commonly and rightly, Christians think of the Lord's Prayer as "Our Father . . ." But a World Communion Sunday sermon on this other prayer of Christ should help disciples to realize anew their communion with God in Christ, and through this communion their fellowship with Christians everywhere.

I. *Our Lord's prayer for himself* (vs. 1-5). As we brood on these words, we realize that this is indeed the Lord's own prayer. The veil before the inner sanctuary is withdrawn. Like the high priest on the Day of Atonement (Lev., ch. 16), our high priest prays first for himself, then for his followers and co-workers, and then for the whole congregation of the new Israel. John, ch. 17, reports not only the consecration prayer of Jesus, but also, as E. F. Scott wrote, "the consecration of the church which already existed germinally in that knot of disciples." The author of *The Bible Reading Fellowship* observed that this prayer suggests that Jesus had at least three circles of prayer. Have we? When we pray, do we concentrate largely on our own needs and wants?

II. *Christ's prayer for his immediate followers* (vs. 6-9). Can we conceive a better summary of Christ's work than the words of

v. 6? He taught and demonstrated what God was like: "I have manifested thy name to the men whom thou gavest me." He called men into the divine society, or, as we would say, he created the church: "Thine they were, and thou gavest them to me, and they have kept thy word."

Note, in vs. 11-12, Christ's intense desire that his followers be kept from evil, and on World Communion Sunday note his reason. Is this not the same concern expressed in the Disciples' Prayer when he taught us to pray, "Lead us not into temptation"? He longs for us to be, not "holy lumps of ice," but radiant possessors of his joy, the joy which is a by-product of the confidence that one is living within God's will. Scholars tell us that the word translated "sanctify" or "consecrate" in v. 19 ("For their sake I consecrate myself, that they also may be consecrated in truth") has a double meaning. As in Jer. 1:5, it may mean to set apart for a special work; it may also mean to dedicate for

...efect. "Both meanings
...s he faces the cross, for
...es."

...ar ones and our closest
...de those of our Elder

...*he church prays for the*
... prayer closes, its scope
... around the planet the
... only, but also for those
...rd" (v. 20). Once again
... of the prayer: it is for
...orary Christian leaders,
... and searchingly: "Our
...*e are already one. . . .*
...ity that may be denied

but cannot be annulled. . . . If two brothers quarrel, the fact that they belong to one family remains."

Complacent Christians need to be faced with the startling truth laid down in v. 23 that unless we become "perfectly one" the world cannot know that Christ is God's answer to their problems and needs. Our failure to demonstrate our unity in Christ is a major stumbling block to winning men everywhere to Christ. As Christ made known God's character and purpose ("I made known to them thy name, and I will make it known"), so we are to make it known through our oneness in him, which will reflect the infinite love with which the Father loved the Son ("that the love with which thou hast loved me may be in them, and I in them"). Do we really believe it? If we do, what are we doing now to help the Spirit to make Christ's prayer come true? What about our co-operative efforts with Christians of other divisions of the church to do God's will in our community?

LAYMEN'S SUNDAY

Let's Abolish the Laity!

Laymen's Sunday (Men and Missions Day) may relieve the parson of preaching to laymen. If he does give a message on these Sundays, let him think of a saying attributed to Elton Trueblood: The ultimate aim of the Christian church (Protestant) is to abolish the laity! "Would that all the Lord's people were prophets . . . !" will be then no vain hope. The "priesthood of all believers" will be exercised. Every Christian a minister is the New Testament as it is the Reformation objective and standard. A sermon on the title "Let's Abolish the Laity" would provoke some puzzled looks, even a quip or two, and perhaps restore a somnolent church member to new life.

WORLD ORDER SUNDAY

"Study in Futility"

The title is Bertrand Russell's. He used it in writing of what he called H-bomb politics. He insisted that the new issue with which the world is faced by the invention of the hydrogen bomb is not the morality of war, or even the morality of this or that method of waging war. "War has always been morally a horror. . . . It is not that war causes death and destruction, for that has always been its purpose. What is new is that war can no longer achieve the aims of any of the belligerents. . . . What the world has to face is that a world war with modern weapons is not merely wicked, but futile."

This wholly new fact, as Russell calls it, ought not to be new to thoughtful Christian citizens of every nation. Centuries ago the Scriptures of the Old and New Testaments declared it. But now, thanks to science and inventiveness, the truth is demonstrable.

Look at the picture in II Sam. 2:12-28. Abner, commanding general for Israel, and Joab, corresponding number in David's forces, face each other across a pool. "Then Abner said to Joab, 'Let the young men get up and have a fight before us.' 'Very well,' said Joab. So the young men got up. . . . Each caught his opponent by the head and stabbed him in the side, so that they all dropped together. . . . That day the fight . . . was most fierce." (Moffatt.) Then followed Abner's flight from the infuriated troops of David. Deploying his men on a hilltop, Abner turned and faced Joab. "Then Abner called to Joab, 'Shall the sword devour for ever? Do you not know that the end will be bitter? How long will it be before you bid your people turn from the pursuit of their brethren?'" This is war, whether fought with primitive weapons, as in the Old Testament story, or with H-bombs or worse. As more than one soldier and peacemaker has observed, leaders start it; young men fight it; even the leaders get sick of it and cry, "Do you not know that the end will be bitter?"

I. *The destructiveness of the sword.* A first point might be the realistic warning made by Bertrand Russell that now the "sword" can devour everything of value on both sides of every "curtain." Destruction of communism would relieve us all. But if we destroy it by the sword, the bomb, or by the kind of war we can let loose, we shall destroy not only communism but every other ordered system, including our own which we cherish so dearly.

II. *The necessity of strength.* If war is now futile for achieving the kind of ends free men rightly desire, this does not mean — unless you are a convinced Christian pacifist — that our Western democracies should reduce our military strength. If we were to grow weak in the eyes of our rivals, their demands would become so intolerable as to make satisfactory negotiations impossible.

III. *Men's minds must change.* To the fairly obvious statement that strength is necessary must be added the positive directive that increasing numbers of men and women must change their ways of thinking and feeling. When Dwight D. Eisenhower, then our allied commander in chief, returned to America immediately after World War II, he put it this way: "You cannot produce peace by hate and a club." In other words, the mentality and method of war must be abandoned. Granted, it's more easily said than done. We Christian preachers notoriously oversimplify and sentimentalize complicated and hard realities. What does such change in our thinking and emotions involve? Deep understanding, support of every United Nations and national Government measure to remove causes of hatred, fear, and conflict, and, above all, patient, undiscourageable Christian love translated into prayer, mutual aids, experiments in supranational friendships, and other practical programs. " Are we willing," asked Bertrand Russell, who stood outside the Christian church, " that Homo sapiens should display his sapience by universal suicide? " " Shall the sword devour for ever? Do you not know that the end will be bitter? " asks one ancient warrior to another. If our answer to the first two questions is " No," we can back up our conviction with deeds, with votes, with our witness to our neighbors and to our Congressional representatives. Does this sound " soft "? Listen to a hardheaded, professedly irreligious thinker of our time: " Armaments, however necessary meanwhile, will not save mankind. If mankind is to be saved, it must be by love of mankind and by wise thinking inspired by that love." Christians know the source and support of such love.

In II Sam. 2:28 is a stirring call to all Christians and men of peace everywhere: " So Joab blew the trumpet; and all the men stopped, and pursued Israel no more, nor did they fight any more." A greater than Joab or any other has sounded forth his trumpet, summoning us to move out of futility into fraternity, justice, and peace.

Peace in the Midst of War

For even when we came into Macedonia, our bodies had no rest but we were afflicted at every turn — fighting without and fear within. But God, who comforts the downcast, comforted us by the coming of Titus.

II CORINTHIANS 7:5-6.

Peace I leave with you; my peace I give to you; not as the world gives do I give to you. Let not your hearts be troubled, neither let them be afraid. JOHN 14:27.

Here is a word to declare to anxious men and women; and this means a majority of our people at almost any time.

I. "*Wrangling outside and anxiety within.*" During World War I a censor told of reading a letter from a British Tommy to his wife. Evidently the good woman's knowledge of her husband's habits, combined with her anxiety for his safety, made her letters something less than soothing. In any case he wrote back: "I wish you'd quit nagging me. Please let me enjoy this war in peace." Who hasn't wished that life, as well as the communists and the anticommunists, the boss, the children, the creditors, those Joneses with whom we're trying to keep up, would quit nagging us? Then there's us! If only the civil war inside our own souls would end! Even the apostle Paul knew it: "When we arrived in Macedonia we had a wretched time with trouble all round us — wrangling outside and anxiety within." We too must find peace in the midst of interior and external warfare.

II. "*But God* . . ." Accept the fact, underscored by Christian faith and experience, that it is God's will that we should have peace "at the center." Whittier's prayer can be answered if we comply with God's conditions: "Drop thy still dews of quietness, till all our strivings cease." It is the will of our Heavenly Father that each of us should have an inward spiritual life so firm and secure that nothing can overthrow it. "In his will is our peace." We must find this interior serenity where we are and in a world that is as it is. In 1951, when James Norman Hall died on a far-off Pacific island, whither he and Charles Nordhoff had gone to find peace after the first global war, a friend, Norman Cousins, wrote: "There are, alas, no South Sea Islands for any of us in 1951!" Nor today.

III. *Peace in the midst of war.* We must accept also the apparently contradictory fact that God's peace must be experienced in the midst of war. As far as we can see, we shall live in a garrison state from now on. God's peace is out of this world, but we find it only in this world. "In the world you have tribulation," said Christ; "but be of good cheer, I have overcome the world" (John 16:33). This Victor over every foe of peace and life abundant bestowed his peace on his followers as he went to the final agonizing battle of Gethsemane and Calvary.

How do we possess Christ's peace?

1. Accept his forgiveness for our own sins, which lead to the guilt that produces the "fear within" and promotes the "fighting without." "Therefore, since we are justified by faith, we have peace with God through our Lord Jesus Christ" (Rom. 5:1).

2. As we receive his reconciliation, we engage in our service of reconciliation. As we have been forgiven, so we must forgive others. As our estrangement has been ended, we must seek to end the estrangement between others.

3. We travel every step of the road today and tomorrow with Christ for Guide, Companion, and Lord. This will arm us against anxiety and the other foes of peace. This will send us to work and pray on behalf of peace for all men—in our church, in our community, through the United Nations and the church universal. For God in Christ calls us:

"Not to the work of sordid selfish saving
Of our own souls to dwell with Him on high,
But to the soldier's splendid, selfless braving,
Eager to fight for righteousness and die.

"Peace does not mean the end of all our striving,
Joy does not mean the drying of our tears;
Peace is the power that comes to souls arriving
Up to the light where God Himself appears."

—*Geoffrey A. Studdert-Kennedy*

REFORMATION SUNDAY

What Protestants Believe and Should Do

Reformation Sunday may well be used by the preacher for a statement of positive Protestantism. The unknown writer of Heb. 10: 19-25 moves from doctrine to practice and from theology into the "practical department." Would you not agree that the theology of this epistle is shaped and colored by a deep pastoral instinct?

He begins by saying three things about the Lord: (1) Jesus is the living way into God's presence. We enter through the veil, by the flesh and by the humanity of Jesus offered to God. As the rent veil of the Temple opened the way into the Holy of Holies, so the rending of our Lord's flesh reveals God's perfect love. (2) Jesus is God's High Priest. He not only shows us the way; he is the Way. He introduces us to the very Presence. (3) Jesus is the one person who can cleanse us from all consciousness of evil. "Our hearts sprinkled clean from an evil conscience and our bodies washed with pure water" (v. 22). His is no external cleansing, but an inward, spiritual purification of thought and desire.

Of course we Christians within the Reformed faith and order believe much more than this; but at the heart of our creed is this high Christology and this conviction concerning the person and work of Christ. Our Lord Jesus, not any institution bearing his name nor yet any human head of the church, means this, and more, to us as to the anonymous New Testament writer whose words we treasure.

The writer lays down three things:

I. *Let us always engage in regular worship.* Not only once weekly, but daily, again and again, we must turn aside, if only for a moment, into God's presence. "Let us approach the presence of God with a heart wherein the truth dwells" (v. 22). Protestants, no less than our Roman Catholic brethren, have a duty of worship. Every Lord's Day is a day of obligation.

II. *Christians must keep a strong grip on what they believe.* Not even if we awoke in hell one black morning should we lose our grip on our Christian faith. "Let us hold fast to the undeviating hope of our creed, for we can rely absolutely on Him who made the promises," is William Barclay's translation of Heb. 10:23.

III. *Let us take thought for the needs of others.* "A selfish Christianity is a contradiction in terms." But this writer leaves nothing to vague piety. He "spells it out" further: (1) We must incite each other to noble living and set an example. A saint is someone in whom Christ stands revealed. A dying soldier of long ago looked up at Florence Nightingale and murmured, "You're Christ to me." (2) We must worship together. A Christian must give up trying to be "a pious particle," a Christian in isolation. (3) We must encourage each other. Moffatt's version of Eliphaz' reluctant tribute to Job (Job 4:4) reads: "Your words have kept men on their feet." Why is it crucially important for Christians to engage in the ministry of encouragement? Because "the Day [is] drawing near." "Let us not abandon our meeting together — as some habitually do — but let us encourage one another, and all the more so as we see the Day approaching." Of course, like all early church thinkers, the writer thought of Christ's final coming. Yet whatever our eschatology, or lack of it, every man and every woman lives with that day approaching. Always it is later than we think. John Wesley said, "In the time given us let us do all the Christian good we can to all the people we can in all the ways we can."

"Wittenberg Is in America Too!"

Sundays in October should have a clear and affirmative word spoken on behalf of the Reformation, historic and continuing. For ideas for the day and the deed, I commend a message delivered from Old South Church pulpit in Boston by Dr. Frederick M. Meek, under the title "Wittenberg Is in America Too!"

"For there is one God, and there is one mediator between God and men, the man Christ Jesus" (I Tim. 2:5).

What is the inheritance we ought to make our own? Here is Dr. Meek's list. He calls them the Wittenberg propositions for our day.

Proposition one: A casually accepted Protestantism is in danger of being submerged in America by the secular life of the day.

Proposition two: The leading that comes to a man *under God* is supreme, in spite of governments and church councils, dogmas and laws.

Proposition three: Protestant people cannot evade their responsibility to know what Protestant belief and experience are.

What are the salient articles of this belief? (1) That a man, in the shared mutual fellowship of the Christian life, has direct access to Almighty God through Jesus, and that God speaks directly to him. (2) That there is a priesthood of all believers. (3) That we have the right of private judgment. (4) That "the just shall live by faith." (5) That the Bible is the Word of God, and that as they read the Word and allow it to speak to them as individual Christians, the Word of God comes to them. (6) That in Jesus is the ultimate and intimate Lord of life, the Head of the church.

No More Apologies

A sermon along the lines of "no more apologies" for either the Reformation or our Protestant position need not send our separated brethren or Orangemen to the barricades. Why not sound a note on positive Protestantism? An entirely right way would be to indicate that a prone position is not likely to prove that we are either alive to the needs of the hour or that we are "effectives" in the church militant.

Here's a text, and it's from the days of blood and thunder: "And the Lord said unto Joshua, Get thee up; wherefore liest thou . . . upon thy face?" (Josh. 7:10). It is one thing to be humble before God, and another to be humble in a craven sense before any man or institution. Not only the opposition when it asserts arrogant claims, but life itself gets people down. God wants men to stand on their feet and move in obedience to his orders and plans. Think of Ezekiel's similar experience, of Saul of Tarsus on the Damascus road, of weak men and women flat on their faces whom the divine Energizer caused to stand up and who thereby counted.

Main points in such a sermon might be: (1) Life does get us down, sometimes flat on our faces. Like Joshua, we may blame God. (2) God tries to persuade us that the safest position to begin with may be on our knees, provided we do not remain there. Enter God: "Arise, why have you thus fallen . . . ?" (3) Throughout the Bible the dialogue on this theme between God and man proceeds (Ezekiel, Paul). (4) To be lifted up, we need only receive his Spirit. To do this is (*a*) to face facts, including the unpleasant ones, and (*b*) to accept God's offer of forgiveness and enabling power. Said the ancient sage Seneca: "All my life I have tried to climb out of the pit of my besetting sins, and I cannot do it, and I never shall, unless a hand is let down to draw me up." We need a Savior, and we have one. (5) Acceptance of the Spirit involves acceptance of the commission which follows commitment.

ALL SAINTS' DAY

Those of us who serve in nonliturgical churches sometimes refer to ourselves as "free churchmen." Rubrics, directives, and other requirements of ecclesiastical leaders are not mandatory for us. As "free churchmen" we are free to observe the great days of the Christian year and free to ignore them. Happily, for a balanced diet of preaching and other acts of corporate worship, more of us exercise our freedom to use the traditional "high days." In October and November occur two such occasions, All Saints' Day and All Souls'. Protestants, at least their small fry, have long observed the eve of All Saints' Day — Allhallows Eve — but usually not as an opportunity for religious observance. We call it Halloween. Then "ghoulies and ghosties and things that go bump in the night" are imagined to be playfully abroad. Is this a survival of a once vivid, perhaps naïve, belief in the proximity of the departed?

In any case, All Saints' Day is for the preacher to witness to a central certitude of the faith: "the communion of saints." Let no thunder from the pagans intimidate us! To emphasize the reality of the unseen, the persistence of personality "in Christ" after death, and the continued growth and fellowship of the Christian community in the church triumphant, is not to divert the living from essential social tasks here and now. Are many American Protestant pulpits guilty of exalting "pie in the sky by and by"?

"A Cloud of Witnesses"

Of course, you have thought of the rich Scripture of Heb. 12:1-2: "Therefore, since we are surrounded by so great a cloud of witnesses, let us also lay aside every weight, and sin which clings so closely, and let us run with perseverance the race that is set before us, looking to Jesus the pioneer and perfecter of our faith, who for the joy that was set before him endured the cross, despising the shame, and is seated at the right hand of the throne of God." The text breaks open as you brood on it.

I. *Our allies*. These are the "cloud of witnesses," the good and faithful of every age and race, those who trusted in God and, as the Te Deum sings, were not "confounded." What of our own dear ones beyond the veil of time and sense? Does it not inspirit and challenge to think of that noble soul with whom in other days we walked and worked as now being in the gallery of heaven — watching us hopefully, "pulling for us"? What of the so-called "former" members of the church? For most congregations the largest number of members are in the church triumphant.

II. *Our action*. To "lay aside every weight, and sin which clings so closely." When Paul asked members of one of the first congregations what now detained them after they had earlier been running well, the honest answer would have been "the weight" of second-rate concerns, the "impedimenta" of secular interests, and the drag of that pride, self-centeredness, and willful disobedience to the law of Christ which the Bible bluntly calls "sin." How do we discard the impending load? John Steinbeck's novel *East of Eden* has a striking passage on a permissible translation of the Hebrew word "*timshel*" in Gen. 4:1-16: "Thou mayest rule over sin." "'Thou mayest'! 'Thou mayest'! What glory!" exclaims one of the healthiest characters in the book. "It is true that we are weak and sick and quarrelsome, but if that is all we ever were, we would, millenniums ago, have disappeared from the face of the earth." The Christian will deepen the truth, which in Steinbeck's view is mainly humanistic, despite its stirring hopefulness.

Stripping the excess baggage from us is not enough: "Let us run with perseverance the race that is set before us." Sinners persevere alarmingly; saints in the making frequently give up at the first obstacle in the course. Saints, said Robert Louis Stevenson, are just those who keep on trying. Our Lord seemed to fear hasty discipleship, since it was so often followed by hasty running away.

III. *Our aim and our attitude.* "Let us run . . . looking to Jesus." Why? Because he is who he is, "pioneer and perfecter of our faith," God-in-a-human-life seated at the right hand of the throne of God — at the center of power. Why? Because he went this way before we did; he was "in all points tempted like as we are, yet without sin" (Heb. 4:15). He endured the worst and yet triumphed. He can help us to finish well, in spite of our frailty and falling.

"Keep Jesus steadily in sight." When we do, we are not distracted; we have the standards of judgment; we have reality, power, assurance of ultimate victory. (Look at v. 3 of ch. 12 in the RSV.)

"The Communion of Saints"

A textual basis may be found in one of Paul's salutations: "To the saints which are at . . ." (Eph. 1:1; Rom. 1:7; I Cor. 1:2; Phil. 1:1).

Plan the sermon by answering two relevant questions:

I. *Who were the saints?* Not only those who are perfect, for Eph. 5:18 contains an admonition asking the saints to go more lightly on the wine. Yet Paul's gracious greeting in Romans is suggestive: "To all God's beloved in Rome, who are called to be saints." The New Testament saints were the committed, those who had responded to God's call in Christ.

II. *What is meant by "the communion of saints"?* Here you may do profitable teaching as to the meaning of the Reformed faith concerning the doctrine. Originally the phrase may have meant communion or fellowship with the perfect and the just in heaven. For Augustine, it was the communion of the good and pious, who love God and one another. Do we not believe that the fellowship of the church is without frontiers and transcends barriers of time and space? Even brief exposition of this neglected doctrine will prove informative to your hearers; it will also provide comfort for those whose hearts carry a little white cross of bereavement. A noble servant of Christ, who had been deprived of the visible presence of his lovely wife, whispered to me after a Communion service, "When I pray she is so near."

Another question never far from tender spirits who mourn the loss of one precious to them could be answered helpfully in such a sermon: Can we pray for the "dead"? Is this part of "communion" with them? Early Christians certainly remembered those who had "gone before," and many daringly believed that the departed ones helped them in God's presence. As unrepentant Protestants we acknowledge the abuses to which this led, but, as the late Ernest Fremont Tittle said, "what is here in question is prayer for the saints and not prayer to the saints, which is another matter. . . . Prayer for those who have gone before is surely in keeping with the Christian faith that when a man dies that is not the end of him."

A little poem that many have found strengthening in its Christian insight begins, "How can I cease to pray for thee?"

Saints of Every Day

The word "saint" is a glorious term for Christians which needs to be rescued both from an impossibly exalted connotation and from a repellent kind of piety which few good people aspire to reproduce. Yet the New Testament insists that men and women like ourselves, folk like those whom we serve in our parishes, are called to be saints. Why not clarify the meaning of the term for our people? Let them see that when Paul speaks of "all God's beloved in Rome, who are called to be saints" (Rom.

1:7) and when he addresses the church of God at Corinth as "those who are consecrated in Christ Jesus, called to be saints" (I Cor. 1:2, Moffatt), he is speaking of garden-variety Christians, morally frail, often pitifully ordinary in their behavior, slipping again and again from the heights of Christian conduct. J. B. Phillips, in his paraphrase, illuminates the meaning memorably: "To you all, the loved of God and called to be Christ's men and women" and "to those whom Christ has made holy [humans can't do it for themselves], who are called to be God's men and women, to all true believers in Jesus Christ, your Lord and ours." Not even the humblest and the most realistic concerning his poor record as a disciple can deny that he has been called to be God's man or woman, or say that he doesn't believe in Christ. He has been dedicated and set apart. This is part of what the Greek word translated "saint" means. Not perfection, but consecration is meant.

Another ray of light on our high vocation as Christians issues from a commonly overlooked fact. In the New Testament the term is always used in the plural. Saintliness is not limited to individuals of special holiness. Here is where we diverge sharply from the Roman Catholic concept of sainthood. To the New Testament church, a solitary saint was a contradiction in terms. Real life—real sainthood—is meeting, praying, toiling, evangelizing, with others in Christ's community. Robinson Crusoe must have at least his man Friday to experience the communion of saints on his island! Therefore, the church in its local expression is essential to spiritual growth; it is a school of saints.

A third emphasis needed by comfortable "saints" was stressed by the Quaker saint, Rufus M. Jones. In his study of *The Luminous Trail* he wrote: "Saints prove that in some hard crisis a person may become the instrument, in divine wisdom, of changing the line of march, and of inaugurating a new time. Not always was it a saint that did it, but it was always a transmitter, and always the trail was luminous." Is this what was meant by the surprising affirmation of Scripture, "The saints are to manage the world"? Manifestly this reminder that a person may become an instrument of the divine purpose whereby mankind moves along a new path on a higher level, helps to answer the questions, What are saints for? To what are we called?

Fruitful also in any study of New Testament sainthood is the insight that the Lord's standard of measurement differs profoundly from ours and from that of official Christianity. Somewhere I heard of a zealous "defender" of the faith who was determined that her fellow members should sing only hymns untainted by heresy. Her pastor asked her to select three that she was sure were orthodox doctrinally. She chose "Was There Ever Kindest Shepherd," "Jesus, the Very Thought of Thee," and "Nearer, My God, to Thee." She did not realize that the first two were by Roman Catholics and the third by a Unitarian. "The Lord knows those who are his," and includes some persons in his company whom we suspect may be unreliable, unimportant, or not quite up to our grade of respectability.

Life Marches On!

But here I am alive.

II CORINTHIANS 6:9 (MOFFATT).

If you prefer more of the context, Phillips' version is striking: "Never far from death, yet here we are alive, always 'going through it' yet never 'going under.'"

If Saint Paul lived today, he would be regarded as a poor life insurance risk. Certainly his application for a sickness and accident policy would be refused. Long before he wrote what we know as the second letter to the Corinthians, he should have given up life's struggle. Recall his catalogue of calamities: "suffering, . . . troubles, . . . calamities, . . . lashes, . . . imprisonment; mobbed, toiling, sleepless, starving." Then follows in his vehement fashion the words, "But here I am alive." It is the defiant chuckle of a brave soul who is keeping his appointment with life. Surrounded by so much that is ephemeral:

1. Stay yourselves, and wonder at the irresistible thrust of life.

Some call it the "life force" and others call it by the simpler, truer name of "God." Too often we surrender to the mood of "Ol' Man River" — "we're scared of livin' and feared of dyin'" and just go limping along. Life, not just its accidents and disasters, is an act of God. Consider the operation of this principle in the world of nature. Prof. J. Arthur Thompson, a scientist from Aberdeen, has said that there are more forms of life in a bucket of sea water than there are stars visible to the naked eye on a clear night. And consider the pilgrimage of life, in spite of fierce enemies, from the amoeba to the living soul!

2. Paul was thinking of the spiritual counterpart. Thanks to God's provision for his human children's needs, thanks to God's gift of Christ whose gift is life abundant, the life-affirming forces are mightier than the life-denying forces, the forces of death. As the writer of The Revelation declares, Christ has "the keys of hell and of death," and he is "alive for evermore."

3. Is this not one of the glorious facts concerning human beings at their best? Knocked down by adversity, cruelly crippled by accident, disease, and handicaps, they rise again and again, their spirits saying, "Here I am alive!" When a great Harvard Medical School teacher continued helping the sick and instructing young medics, despite his own incurable malignant disease, one who knew him best said: "He has become to us who knew him the most powerful and convincing evidence for personal and family religion that we have ever seen. Death has no more dominion over him."

4. Could we not take courage from the fact that institutions and movements, which we believe are blessed by God, have the future with them because this principle operates in them and for them? Think of the many attempts to devise and keep working systems of collective security. There have been twenty-six attempts at some form of united nations organization before the present one! Of each one we could say, as historians have said, "Dying, and behold it lives." Noteworthy is the Christian church. Crucified like its founder and Lord, it emulates him because his life is in it, and rises reborn, stronger.

5. Can we say this honestly concerning those dear and good souls who have vanished from our sight because of physical death? We can, if they were "in Christ," says the New Testament. Whatever we make of general immortality, it is an integral article of Christian faith that the human personality God has made and redeemed, committed to him in trust and obedience through this phase of life, will survive the physical extinction of the body and go on toward perfection in the next dimension of life. Who knows? Perhaps that loved one whom we so sorely miss is even now quietly chuckling—if the ears of the spirit could only catch it, "But here I am alive!" Said Socrates on the eve of his death, "Bury me if you can catch me!" Said a dying British prime minister, Bonar Law, to a younger colleague: "Good-by, Asquith, I'll see you again. This is not the last of me." Said the Lord of life, "I will come again." Here I am alive!

STEWARDSHIP DAY

Fares, Please

Stewardship is an expression of discipleship to be emphasized every Sunday. However, on one Sunday each year most pastors are expected to deliver a " special message " on this theme. If you have not done so, try a sermon on the text in Jonah 1:3, " So he paid the fare, and went on board." True, he shouldn't have been on that ship. His orders designated Nineveh as destination, and this ship was sailing to Tarshish. He was not the last deliberately to take the wrong boat. More than one man has " found a ship going to Tarshish . . . away from the presence of the Lord." But at least he paid the fare. Indeed, before that voyage was over he paid more than he had dreamed would be necessary.

After such an honest look at the context, you should be able to lift the word up into other relationships. All is of grace; the best of life is given us — life itself, our dearest, our friends, our Savior. But the once-popular song " The Best Things in Life Are Free " is only half true. We can't get to heaven in a rocking chair; indeed, ministers realize they can't get to heaven on clergy fare!

" Freely ye have received, freely give " is also Christian. When it comes to maintaining the ship of the Spirit, providing the cargo for the export business of the Christian enterprise, underwriting the crew, and supporting Christ's representatives in distant, difficult outposts, do we pay our fare? Do we travel on a " pass," or want to be treated as children, being carried at half fare? " He paid the fare, and went on board."

How to Handle Our Debts

Pay all of them their dues, taxes to whom taxes are due, revenue to whom revenue is due, respect to whom respect is due, honor to whom honor is due. Owe no one anything, except to love one another; for he who loves his neighbor has fulfilled the law.

ROMANS 13:7-8.

Paul's insistence on civil obedience is essentially sound, even when we do not completely share his religious attitude toward the state, and even when the wielder of state power is a Nero. No Christian — indeed, no man — can dissociate himself from the society in which he lives. We cannot resign from this ship, however much we disagree with the skipper, the officers, or the arrangements. As a member of the nation, each citizen enjoys privileges which he cannot claim if, at the same time, he refuses the duties. "He is bound up in the bundle of life; as he is part of the body of the church, he is also part of the body of the nation. There is no such thing in this world as an isolated individual. A man has a duty to the state and must discharge that duty" — even if a tyrant is on the throne. Whether Government administrators know it or not, they do God's work in helping to preserve their part of the world from chaos. A Christian owes them a debt; it is a part of Christian duty to help to repay this debt by helping and not hindering.

You could clarify for yourself, if not for your hearers, the basis of Paul's demand for civil obedience. You could indicate how, carried to extreme lengths, this view would cause Christians to rationalize their support of a Hitler rather than encourage their resistance to such a representative of Antichrist. Direct transition to the main theme would be some pertinent reference to debts, national, church, and personal. Few persons are without firsthand acquaintance with the dismal business.

Then proceed to define (1) public debts and (2) private debts. Verse 7 mentions two of the public debts: the public debt Paul calls "tribute," or "taxes." Tribute is the amount of money or service that must be paid by members of a subject nation. Apparently Roman authorities levied three such tributes on their captive or defeated subjects: ground tax (one tenth of all grain, one fifth of all wine and fruit produced on his ground); income tax (one per cent of a man's income); and the poll tax (paid by everyone between the ages of fourteen and sixty-five). By "revenue," Paul meant local taxes. It might be comforting to twentieth-century taxpayers to be reminded of the number imposed by ancient Rome: custom duties; import and export taxes; taxes for use of highways, for crossing bridges, for entry into markets and harbors, for right to possess an animal; as well as operator's tax to drive cart or wagon.

Then Paul turns to private debts. Is this a counsel of a perfectionist: "Owe no one anything"? Far from it; it is the way to live satisfactorily, if you can manage it. Some early disciples of the Lord assumed that you couldn't manage it, and that you didn't need to worry much if you couldn't! Hence they twisted the petition in the Lord's Prayer, "Forgive us our debts, as we forgive our debtors," to mean absolution from all financial obligations and other debts. So Paul reminded his people that being a Christian does not excuse anyone for welshing on his obligations. It means that we have the highest reason for fulfilling our obligations to the last full measure.

But there is one debt that a man must go on paying every day which he can never hope or even want to have marked, "Paid in full." This is the debt to love one another. Origen, the early church father and teacher, put it this way: "The debt of love remains with us permanently and never leaves us; this is a debt that we both discharge every day and forever owe." We are to keep trying to pay this debt, even while we realize that it is unpayable. Could you not do something with this principle of Christian living in relation to church support as one expression of our obligation? Lifting this up to the height of Christian stewardship, must we not keep saying that since we are bought with a price and are divinely loved creatures, we must give our utmost to the highest? One practical way of doing this is at least to begin operating on the Old Testament tithe level and move up and over into the New Testament realm of grace. "We love, because he first loved us." "God so loved . . . that he gave." "Love so amazing, so divine, demands" — a dollar a week? two dollars? five? fifteen per cent as deductible from income tax? or "my life, my soul, my all"?

For another approach, using the same passage, consult a Bible concordance for the word "debtor." It is used by Paul at least three times in as many different contexts. You may find that this triple emphasis offers a structure for your message that your people will remember and act upon.

THANKSGIVING SUNDAY

How's your logopedics? or, rather, how are you in logopedics? You never heard of it? You detect no symptoms yet? I never heard of it until an advertisement appeared in an issue of a Canadian weekly, *Saturday Night*. A South African university advertised for a senior lecturer in "logopedics." The minimum qualification for the position is a Ph.D. in logopedics. As the trapper who had been bushed for several years in the subarctic remarked when he used the telephone on one of his rare visits to the trading post, what will they think of next? Dictionaries don't help much in defining the word. From its roots you might think it means "the kicking around of words," and Webster knows we do that enough. A speech expert came to the rescue. Logopedics, he volunteered, is also known as lalopathology and has to do with teaching people how to speak properly — "correcting difficulties in speech, removing word blocks, and so on." Then I learned that the University of Iowa gives a course leading to a degree in logopedics. I resist any temptation to excoriate ourselves as speakers for doing what the obvious and incorrect meaning of the term suggests — kicking words around. Much of the world's trouble comes from widespread and sometimes malicious abuse of great words — freedom, democracy, faith, love, and others.

But November reminds us of one noble word that comes in for considerable punishment, either from glib use or from neglect of it — "thanks." This month of frost on the pumpkin (in the northeast), of football finals, feasting, and its aftermath of flatulence, comes to a peak with our most American festival, Thanksgiving. It is not only our uniquely American contribution to the civil and Christian year's celebrations; it also expresses the most characteristic note of Christian prayer and devotion.

Dr. Arthur John Gossip, in his golden manual on the devotional life, *In the Secret Place of the Most High,* has a chapter on this theme in which he makes a convincing and eloquent case for giving thanksgiving the chief place on the list. Saints and liturgical scholars might demur; adoration is considered by them as the highest form of prayer and spiritual activity. Yet is a man moved to adore if he knows not the emotion of gratitude? "Thanks be to thee for thy unspeakable gift!" exclaims the adoring recipient to the divine Giver.

Gilbert K. Chesterton, writing of Saint Francis of Assisi, wrote succinctly: "The great painter boasted that he mixed all his colors with brains, and the great saint may be said to mix all his thoughts with thanks." Certainly in more than one language "think" and "thank" are closely related. There may be a germinal idea for a sermon in that kinship.

Taken for Granted

Weren't there ten men healed? Where are the other nine? Is nobody going to turn and praise God for what has been done, except this stranger? LUKE 17:18 (PHILLIPS).

Was no one found to return and give praise to God except this foreigner? (RSV).

I. "*Forgetful Green.*" Many towns and villages have their public commons or greens. This is notably the case in New England. The local green is useful as well as decorative. But one authority on human traffic problems found one green that ought to be surrounded with warning signs. John Bunyan located "Forgetful Green." You can find the story in Part II of *The Pilgrim's Progress.* Christian had his battle with Apollyon "in a narrow passage, just beyond Forgetful Green. And indeed that place is the most dangerous place in all these parts. For if at any time the pilgrims meet with any brunt, it is when they forget what favors they have received, and how unworthy they are of them."

A greater guide than Bunyan voiced astonishment that so many stray to Forgetful Green. Here retell the story of Jesus and the ten lepers. "Where are the other nine?" On Forgetful Green. Samuel Leibowitz, famous criminal lawyer, saved seventy-eight men from the electric chair. How many took the trouble to thank their deliverer? None.

II. *Beware of forgetting.* We have been warned many times in Scripture: "Beware lest thou forget all the way the Lord thy God had led thee" (Deut. 6:12). Jesus before the cross remembered and was grateful: "Father, I thank thee." The sign of the cross is a symbol and reminder that:

III. *The major element in life is the given.* Christianity's chief act of worship has for one of its titles, "Eucharist"—thanksgiving. What of the unearned increment of life? in our cultural and national heritage? in family life? in our friendships?

IV. *The way out.* If you and I dawdle on Forgetful Green, mope in depression, moan in complaint, what is the way out and up? Psalm 103 has the formula: "Forget not all his benefits: who forgiveth all thy sin, and healeth all thine infirmities; who saveth thy life from destruction, and crowneth thee with mercy and loving-kindness." Do we take God for granted and treat casually redemption and loving care all the days of our years? Where are the nine, the nine hundred, the nine thousand, being cleansed and nourished and kept by the divine love and mercy? Only 10 per cent turn back praising God and giving him thanks. But you and I could be one of that saving minority.

"Lord, thou hast given so much.
Give one thing more,
A grateful heart."

— *George Herbert*

The Shortest Way to Happiness

A topic such as this should have reader appeal. Who does not want to be happy, even when moralists condemn the quest? John Q. Citizen and his wife and children look up into the face of the sky and ask, sometimes petulantly, sometimes defiantly, often beseechingly, "Please, may we enjoy life?" Devious are the routes explored, and not a few prove to be dead ends. Your introduction may acknowledge the ceaseless search, the main trails followed by twentieth-century travelers eager to enjoy what the founding fathers claimed to be one of man's inalienable rights, "the pursuit of happiness."

What is the shortest, surest route? Two centuries ago a wise and good Englishman gave a direction that surprises us. It occurs in the classic he bequeathed to the race, a book with the forbidding title *A Serious Call to a Devout and Holy Life*. (John Wesley acknowledged his indebtedness to this book, saying that it sowed the seed of Methodism.) Here is William Law's answer to our question, What is the shortest way to happiness?

"If anyone tell you the shortest, surest way to all happiness and all perfection, he must tell you to make a rule to yourself to thank and praise God for everything that happens to you. For it is certain that whatever seeming calamity happens to you, if you thank and praise God for it, you turn it into a blessing."

However naïve and absurd we think that claim may be, we must admit that it is on the main line of the New Testament emphasis, and of the Old Testament too, when the latter reports its most spiritual insights. Here is the apostle Paul, writing to Thessalonian Christians (I Thess. 5:18): "In every thing give thanks: for this is the will of God in Christ Jesus concerning you." The RSV expresses it tersely: "Give thanks in all circumstances; for this is the will of God in Christ Jesus for you." My choice of translation would be that of Dr. Edgar J. Goodspeed: "Thank God whatever happens. For this is what God through Jesus Christ wants you to do." Here is a text for the sermon.

I. *The duty of thankfulness.* Is this not too simple a rule for happiness? How can any rational person, realistically aware of the tragedies and frustrations, the ills and accidents of life, give thanks "whatever happens"? Why should he? How can thanksgiving in unpleasant situations issue in happiness? What is the alternative? Complaining, whimpering, whining are common ones. Stoical endurance of what can't be cured is a less frequent attitude.

That foe of sin and friend of sinners, the famous Edinburgh divine Alexander Whyte, once visited a woman of his parish. She delivered to her minister a long litany of woe, and a bill of complaints, with all and sundry the targets. Dr. Whyte listened patiently and attentively to the end. Doubtless some of the charges made by the disgruntled soul were justified. As he prepared to leave her home, he prescribed the treatment: "Mind you," he said, "'Forget not all his benefits.'" It is likely the good woman, being a Scots Presbyterian of that particular generation, could complete the quotation: "forget not all his benefits: who forgiveth all thy sin, and healeth all thine infirmities; who saveth thy life from destruction, and crowneth thee with mercy and loving-kindness" (Ps. 103:2-4). Here, then, is your second emphasis, accenting the positive.

II. "*Have you anything to declare?*" When beset by despondencies, follow this rule of the road: Take a walk among your mercies. Very exceptional is the person who tries this exercise and does not find that blessings outnumber their opposite.

> "There are nettles everywhere,
> But tall green grasses are more common still,
> The blue of heaven is larger than the cloud."

If you reflect and recollect, you will find yourself moving on the road to happiness.

Crossing the U.S.-Canadian border, every traveler hears a question invariably asked by a customs official, "Have you anything to declare?" Well, have we? Is there nothing in our mental and spiritual luggage to declare with thanksgiving? Robert Louis

Stevenson was certain that "the man who has forgotten to be thankful has fallen asleep in life."

A high school commencement speaker awakened his audience by saying that the worst "ism" prevalent among us is not communism, or fascism, but somnambulism. People who walk around in their sleep, not knowing what life is all about and not caring, are subversive of the nation's spiritual welfare and of their own.

"Have you anything to declare"—gratefully?

Here would be the place in which to indicate a few of "all the blessings of this life": the old sweet fashions of nature, seed-time, summer, and harvest, "purple mountain majesties" and tawny prairies; a land where freedom and justice and everyone's security are real and regnant; home love and life, and the companionship of friends; work, if it is socially useful and satisfying; children, with their needs and promise. It all sounds positively lyrical, snorts the cynic. And is there no place for a lyrical interlude amid the strident sounds of the world's *miserere?* Can we not thank God also for life in this era of volcanic change and yet of creative change also? Polycarp, Christian martyr of the year 155, exclaimed, "My God! in what a century you have caused me to live!" We can make that cry ours, without recoiling in horror or slithering in self-pity. "Now God be thanked who matched us with his hour!" shouted Rupert Brooke in the midst of world war.

Should we not thank God for life in the midst of unending war against demonic forces, and for a chance to join the ranks of those determined to defeat hunger and disease, hatred, fear, and injustice? And what of our great and gracious God? "In every thing" there is his love and purpose, his mighty acts of redemption in the Lord Jesus Christ. "Have you anything to declare?" What of the world-wide church, of its rediscovery as the great new fact of our time? Who can exhaust the list of what we can and should declare with "humble and hearty thanks"?

III. *The grace to be thankful.* But this is not what William Law had in mind. So we come to the next point. Our spiritual director in his famous book said that to travel the "shortest, surest way to all happiness" we must "make it a rule to thank and praise God for everything that happens to us." For everything? For broken hopes that are our pillows some nights? For little crosses which mark the graves of our dearest? For the disasters of life? Yes, insist the masters of the art of Christian living, for everything, and in everything. Praise and service are great healers. Is this impossibly high? Perhaps, until we come across a man praying with the shadow of a cross enveloping his kneeling figure. "At that time," says Matthew (ch. 11:25) — when many of his own people had rejected him when he foresaw the ruin inevitably following their disobedience to God's purpose — "at that time Jesus answered and said, I thank thee, O Father, Lord of heaven and earth, because thou hast hid these things from the wise and prudent, and hast revealed them unto babes." And when the hounds of hell were yelping at his heels, and death on the cross was now the only way to fulfill God's design in man's dreadful disorder, "the Lord Jesus, the same night in which he was betrayed, took bread: and when he had given thanks, he brake it, and said, Take, eat" (I Cor. 11:23). Ever since, we call the observance of that supper of sacrifice the Eucharist, the thanksgiving. Will you ever forget hearing of that incredibly heroic family of missionaries, the Lees of India? When six of their household were buried in a landslide at Darjeeling, the others built a monument. On it the desperately bereaved parents inscribed the New Testament words, "Thanks be to God, which giveth us the victory through our Lord Jesus Christ."

We have a duty of thankfulness. We have so much to declare. But only God himself can give us the grace to be thankful in everything and in all circumstances. This grace he furnishes, "exceeding abundantly above all that we ask or think." We must take it and use it. Such gracious thankfulness may even bring other wounded persons back to life's front line again, healed, fortified, and eager to do their part in the great cause.

Is there something here that pagans and pessimists never

know? Let them take the long road, and we'll take the short road. It is entirely possible that we'll be in heaven before them, for have we not high authority for believing that the Kingdom of heaven is within us?

Reasons for Gratitude

Psalm 116:7-8, 17 provides basis, background, and specific reasons for gratitude. A title might be that of the invitation I once saw on an old country roadside bench: "Rest and be thankful."

A brilliant English lay preacher once preached on what he called "Holy Harvest." He used the unusual text of I Sam. 6:13. Farmers and city dwellers alike would be struck with its apposite and picturesque quality. Don't overlook the people of Bethshemesh "reaping their wheat harvest"!

Once I used two texts from The Psalms (Ps. 78:19 and Ps. 23:5): "Can God furnish a table in the wilderness?" and "Thou preparest a table before me in the presence of mine enemies." Imaginatively reconstruct the setting and the mood of the people to which the writer of Ps. 78 transmitted his word of God.

INDEXES

INDEXES

Names and Subjects

Scripture References